"...  ollection of lite   ow God reveal   istorical events,   . Too much emphasis cannot be given to the oft-repeated statement that the Old Testament is the story of God's action, describing what he has done, what he is doing, and what he will yet do. Only as one studies the Old Testament from that viewpoint can he get insight into its meaning."

DR. ADAM W. MILLER, dean emeritus of the graduate School of Theology of Anderson College, is a renowned Bible scholar and author of INTRODUCTION TO THE NEW TESTAMENT and BRIEF INTRODUCTION TO THE NEW TESTAMENT. A former missionary, Dr. Miller has traveled extensively in the Middle East where he has traced at first hand the path of events described in this book.

INTRODUCTION TO
THE
OLD
TESTAMENT

(ORIGINAL TITLE: BRIEF INTRODUCTION TO THE
OLD TESTAMENT)

Adam W. Miller

THE WARNER PRESS
Anderson, Indiana

This *Introduction to the Old Testament* has been prepared in response to requests for a book on the part of ministers and church school workers that would serve as a companion volume to the *Brief Introduction to the New Testament.*

It is designed primarily for use in connection with study courses on the Old Testament for church workers, although it will have wider use as an elective course in the church school, in-service ministerial training institutes, and for individual study. For this reason critical discussions have been eliminated as much as possible.

We hope that this companion volume about the Old Testament will be instrumental in creating a greater appreciation and study and understanding of God and his word as we have it in the Old Testament.

THE PUBLISHERS

Scripture quotations unless otherwise credited are from the Revised Standard Version of the Holy Bible, copyright, 1952, by the Division of Christian Education, NCCCUSA, and are used by permission.

INTRODUCTION TO THE OLD TESTAMENT
(orig. title: BRIEF INTRODUCTION TO THE OLD TESTAMENT)

A PORTAL BOOK
Published by Pillar Books for Warner Press, Inc.

Portal Books edition published May 1976

ISBN: 0-87162-193-2

Library of Congress Catalog Number: 64-11424

Copyright © 1964 by Warner Press, Inc.

All Rights Reserved

Printed in the United States of America

PORTAL BOOKS are published by Warner Press, Inc.
1200 East 5th Street, Anderson, Indiana 46011, U.S.A.

CONTENTS

A BRIEF INTRODUCTION TO THE OLD TESTAMENT

INTRODUCTION

PART IV. THE WRITINGS

INTRODUCTION

CHAPTER I

WHAT IS THE OLD TESTAMENT?

The Old Testament is not a single book, but a collection of books. It is not the work of one man, but of a number of writers extending over a period of not less than a thousand years. This means that the Old Testament grew from book to book, century after century, until our present collection of thirty-nine books was complete.

But the Old Testament is more than a collection of literary writings. It is the record of how God revealed himself in historical events covering a long period of history. In those events God is seen at work carrying out his purpose and revealing his nature and his attributes by what he does. Those great events recorded in the literature of the Old Testament are all related to God's redemptive action in which we see God at work among the Hebrew people in order to bring about their salvation and the salvation of the whole world. It is this revelation which God makes of himself and of his purpose for mankind that ties together in a unified whole, all of the books of the Old Testament. The Old Testament story from beginning to end is the historical action of God. In it he seeks reconciliation—between man and God, the human and the divine, the creature and the creator.

Behind the life and literature of the Old Testament are the fundamental beliefs of the people of Israel, established early in their history. Before the literature came into existence, God's action and dealings with

Israel, through which he revealed himself and his purpose, had given them these fundamental and distinctive elements of faith. The Mosaic faith, upon which the entire Old Testament rests, contains three basic elements:

(1) History was the revelation of God. This meant that Yahweh was the God who acted in history. For them history "moved without haste and without rest to His appointed goal." This faith in Yahweh stood in contrast with the false gods, the idols of wood and stone of the ancient world, which could do nothing and could not save. This idea of the living active God was quite different from the Greek idea of God who did not act at all. This idea the Hebrews met late in their history. The Greek idea suggested that once God had set all things in motion nothing more need be done. He turns his back upon the world and waits for all things to be drawn towards him. But such a God is not one who can hear, can answer, can act, and can save.

(2) God himself had taken the initiative in selecting the Israelites as his special people and in making a covenant with them. They had not chosen him; he had chosen them. The Hebrew community and their relationship to Yahweh was based on this covenant. They were the people of God through whom the revelation was to be given to the world.

(3) There is only one God. Their faith in Yahweh as the God who acts in history meant that he alone controlled the events and the course of history.

H. Wheeler Robinson tells of a manuscript of the Hebrew Bible in one of our great libraries, "beautifully written, but having an ugly brown stain on the first and last pages of the Pentateuch. The stain is blood shed in some massacre of the Jews and looting of the synagogues. Perhaps it represents the loyalty of a life given in defense of the book. It needs such a loyalty to maintain a religion, but it needs loyalty certainly not less to beget it. The famous words of Milton about great literature are truest of all when they are applied to the literature of the Old Testament—'the precious life-blood of a master spirit, embalmed and treasured up on purpose to a life beyond life.' "¹ The Old Testament is just such literature, literature which reveals how God spoke to his ancient people through stirring events, and through which he continues to speak to us today.

SECTION 1. THE OLD TESTAMENT STORY

To understand the Old Testament and its message, it is essential to have some knowledge of the Old Testament story as a whole. The story—for the most part the story of God at work among a particular people, beginning with the family of Abraham about nineteen hundred and fifty years before Christ—covers the history of Israel down to the time of the Maccabees, one hundred and sixty-seven years before the coming of Christ.

1. *The Prologue.* The story begins with what has been called primeval history, contained in Genesis, chapters 1-11. It takes the reader back to the beginning of all things and thus gives to the history of the Hebrews the larger setting of general human history from the beginning. It opens with the story of the creation of heaven and earth and all that is therein. It accounts for the beginning of the families of the earth and reveals how they are related to each other as a result of God's creative act. It tells of the sin of man and its consequences; in fact, the tragedy of sin in the very beginning is the prelude to the whole story, which is the story of God's redeeming acts in history.

2. *The Selection of a Particular People.* Out of all the peoples of the world God selected one man, Abraham, to become the father of this particular people. Abraham migrated from Ur of Chaldea to the region of

¹H. Wheeler Robinson, *The Old Testament, Its Making and Meaning* (Cokesbury, 1937), p. 11.

Haran in northwestern Mesopotamia sometime between 2000 and 1950 B.C. Albright suggests the third quarter of the twentieth century before Christ. From Haran he went to Canaan, stopping first at Shechem. Abraham, Isaac, and Jacob, along with their families and servants roamed the hill country of Canaan. When a famine arose in the land, Jacob and his family went down into Egypt. The conditions at first were favorable for these Hebrews, but later, as a result of a change in the ruling dynasty, persecution set in and conditions for the Hebrews became unbearable.

3. *The Exodus: The Basic and Decisive Event.* The deliverance from bondage in Egypt and the making of the covenant between God and his chosen people constitute the decisive and crucial event in Old Testament history. This is the basic event in Old Testament revelation observed annually in the Feast of the Passover. It was the event which made them a people of destiny in the redemptive purpose of God.

Moses became the leader who led the Hebrews out of Egyptian bondage, an event which took place in either the fourteenth or thirteenth century B.C. (The date is a matter of considerable discussion and will be considered in the next chapter.) Through a series of extraordinary and miraculous events, climaxed by the mighty act at the Red Sea, the Israelites were delivered and journeyed into the desert. There they were molded into a community of free people with a sense of divine destiny. At Sinai a covenant was made which bound the tribes to God as his people, and they became a community with a single religious allegiance.

4. *The Invasion of Canaan.* The stern discipline of the wilderness life prepared the Hebrews for the conquest of Canaan and the problems they were to face upon entering the land. It was under the leadership of Joshua that the Israelites invaded Canaan and claimed the land as their own. Canaan was strategically located in the ancient world, at the very crossroads of the na-

tions. There the Israelites, recipients of the revelation from God, found themselves involved in the life of many of the nations of the world. For a thousand years this historical drama which involved the Hebrews with many of the nations, and within which God revealed himself and his purposes again and again, was to continue to unfold, until in the fullness of time Christ would come as the fulfillment of what had been promised in God's revealing acts.

5. *The Twelve-Tribe Confederacy and the Nation.* The story of the chosen people as a nation begins with the tribal organization set up by Joshua. They were bound together by a common religious bond. There was a central sanctuary at which they worshiped. Although the bond that united these tribes was primarily religious, in times of emergency they combined to fight a common enemy. This type of organization continued through the period of Judges, when the Hebrews had to wage continuous war to defend themselves against their enemies. Later they formed a monarchy to enable them to better stand against the opposition of their enemies. Saul was the first king. He was followed by David and Solomon, and during their reigns Canaan constituted the Hebrew empire.

6. *Disruption of the Kingdom and the Exile.* The kingdom was divided upon the death of Solomon, the two divisions being known as the kingdoms of the north and the south, or Israel and Judah. Located as these kingdoms were in a strategic position between Egypt and Mesopotamia, they were drawn into the struggle for power and ascendancy on the part of these great powers. The Northern Kingdom fell to Assyria in 721 B.C. and the Southern Kingdom fell to the Babylonians with the fall of Jerusalem in 587 B.C. The Temple was destroyed; the people were impoverished and carried away to Babylon in exile. Destruction of the nation was now complete. God's plan for his chosen people seemed defeated.

7. *The Restoration.* But God had a purpose for his people which went back to Abraham and Moses. The Persian Empire that succeeded Babylon, was benevolent in its rule and soon permitted the Hebrews to return to their homeland. Under the leadership of Zerubbabel, Haggai and Zechariah, and later under Ezra and Nehemiah, the Temple and the city of Jerusalem were rebuilt and restoration took place.

The Persian Empire was followed by the Greek rule of Palestine as a result of the conquests of Alexander the Great in 332 B.C. The rulers of Palestine sought to impose Greek religion and culture upon the Jews, which led finally to the Maccabean revolt in 167 B.C. For about one hundred years the Jews had their independence, but with the rise of Rome, Palestine came under the rule of that empire in 63 B.C.

As has already been pointed out, the Old Testament is more than a collection of literary writings. It is the record of how God revealed himself, principally through historical events. As such it is sacred history. Too much emphasis cannot be given to the oft-repeated statement that the Old Testament is the story of God's action, describing what he has done, what he is doing, and what he will yet do. Only as one studies the Old Testament from that viewpoint can he get insight into its meaning.

SECTION 2. THE ORIGIN OF THE OLD TESTAMENT WRITINGS

1. *Before the Old Testament.* We have become so familiar with the Old Testament, its heroes and its stories, its prophets and their great messages, its poetry and its songs, that it is strange to think of a time when there was no Old Testament. But like all other literature, the Old Testament had a beginning.

Before the first book of the Old Testament was written, it seems certain that the Hebrews told of God's dealings with them, or expressed their joy and thanksgiving over some happy experience in stories, poems, and songs. It is likely that the first Hebrew writings were these songs and poems and stories, rather than history or law. But even before these stories and songs were written down, they were chanted or sung, or told again and again in families and groups. They were handed down thus from mouth to ear, from generation to generation. We call this oral transmission. Those familiar with New Testament study will recall that the content of the gospel was preserved in the early churches by this same method of handing down the teachings of Jesus and the story of what he did by word of mouth, until the time came when those things were written down as the beginnings of our written Gospels.

In a similar manner the materials of the Old Testament were kept alive and preserved within the Hebrew community until they were embodied in the books we have today. Out under the stars the sheepherders camped. Their day's work finished, the interval before going to sleep found them resting near the campfire, telling stories of the day's happenings. Often they listened to one of their number who had a talent for recalling the deeds of the past and for telling them dramatically. In that way they kept fresh in the mind the events which made the nation great and through which God had revealed himself.

2. *Fragmentary Accounts.* Literature begins when these stories and songs are written down and embodied in books. Some of those first accounts must have been very short, but in them the people kept alive the rich treasures of what God had spoken and of what he had done. Afterwards these smaller or fragmentary accounts were taken up into larger narratives, or were the source materials for the fuller accounts.

The oldest fragment of Hebrew writing is said to be the following poem, found in Genesis 4:23-24, and referred to as *The Song of the Sword:*

Ada and Zillah, hear my voice;
    you wives of Lamech, harken to what I say:
I have slain a man for wounding me,
    a young man for striking me.
If Cain is avenged sevenfold,
    truly Lamech seventy-sevenfold.

That song sings of a time before there was a Hebrew nation or a Hebrew language, and long before Moses gave the Law with its high moral ideals.

Another bit of ancient poetry is *The Song of the Well,* found in Numbers 21:17:

Spring up, O well! Sing to it!—
the well which the princes dug,
which the nobles of the people delved,
with the scepter and with their staves.

In a semidesert country like Palestine, the discovery of water was always something to be celebrated with music and song, and there was the recognition of the good providence of God who had provided the water.

There are a number of other examples of these early songs. In Genesis 9:25-27 we have *The Sayings of Noah;* in the entire forty-ninth chapter there is *The Song of Jacob's Blessing;* in Exodus 15:1-8 is to be found *The Song of the Red Sea;* and in the fifth chapter of Judges we have *The Song of Deborah.*

Some of the early stories do not appear in the form of poetry. In the account of the heavenly visitors to Abraham (Gen. 18), we have an illustration of this type of early story. Other examples are *The Story of Isaac's Marriage* (chap. 24), *Jacob's Cunning* (chap. 30), *The Offering Up of Isaac* (chap. 22), and *Jacob at Bethel* (chap. 28). These stories all contain significant teaching and form part of that total record in which is revealed God's will and purpose.

3. *Completed Books and Groups of Books.* The next stage in the development of the Old Testament was the writing of the individual books. There are

thirty-nine of these books in the Old Testament. Later they were assembled or brought together as groups of books or as collections of books. The Hebrews divided these books into three groups: the Law, the Prophets, and the Writings.

(1) *The Law or the Pentateuch.* The name *Pentateuch,* which comes from the Greek, refers to the "five-roll" book commonly called the Torah, or the Law. It includes the first five books of our Old Testament: Genesis, Exodus, Leviticus, Numbers, and Deuteronomy. This is the oldest collection of the books of the Old Testament. The Hebrews regarded these five books as a single unit. Just when the divisions into five books took place is not known, but the divisions had already taken place when the Old Testament was translated from Hebrew into Greek about 250 B.C.

This five-roll book is made up of both history and law. The history covered in the Pentateuch begins with what is commonly called "Primeval History." This history comprises the first eleven chapters of Genesis and have sometimes been called the prologue to the story of Abraham. These chapters start with the account of the Creation, and end with the story of the Tower of Babel (Gen. 11:9). From there on begins the story of Abraham and the Patriarchs, the real beginning of Israelite history, ending with the death of Moses (Deut. 34). However, that history contained within the Pentateuch is only the first part of a continuous history of the Hebrew people found within the Old Testament, which carries the reader into the Greek period.

The "five-roll" book is called the Law because it contains the laws commonly referred to as the "Law of Moses." Those laws were the cornerstone of the religion of Israel. No one could be a faithful and devout Jew without studying them.

(2) *The Prophets.* Some time after this first collection was made, a second group of books or collection appeared. The Hebrews call this second group the

Prophets. This collection was divided into two parts, the first part known as the Former Prophets, including Joshua, Judges, the two Books of Samuel and the two Books of Kings; the second part known as the *Latter Prophets,* including Isaiah, Jeremiah, Ezekiel, and the Book of the Twelve (comprising the twelve minor prophets). These books included the historical writings, sermons, and messages of such men as Elijah, Amos, Isaiah, Jeremiah, Ezekiel, and the others who so gloriously interpreted the will and purpose of God for the Hebrew people. Because they did, the Hebrews called all of these books *Prophets.*

(3) *The Writings.* A third collection of books emerged later. This collection contained all of the other canonical books not included in the Law and the Prophets. It was divided into four parts or smaller groups. They were: (1) Psalms, Proverbs, and Job; (2) the "Five Scrolls," namely the Song of Solomon, Ruth, Lamentations, Eccelesiastes, and Esther; (3) the Book of Daniel; (4) Ezra-Nehemiah (listed as one book), and the two Books of Chronicles.

SECTION 3. THE OLD TESTAMENT CANON

The Old Testament as we know it in the printed editions of our English Bible contains thirty-nine books. These represent only a portion of the religious writings that appeared among the Hebrew people before the New Testament times. It was from among this body of writings that the thirty-nine books we now know as the Old Testament were selected and recognized as authoritative. Why was it that some books were included while others were excluded? What was the basis of selection? What was the principle for determining whether a book should or should not be accepted as authoritative? These are some of the questions usually asked in a study of the Old Testament Canon.

1. *Meaning of the Term "Canon."* This English word is derived from the Greek word *kanōn*, which in the Hebrew is *qaneh*. The root meaning of the word is "reed." Since the reed was very early used as a means of measuring, the word soon came to mean a measuring rod. When this word was applied to the books of the Bible, it meant that any book judged to be in harmony with a certain standard or "measured up" to that standard, was accepted as authoritative for belief and conduct. Such a book was considered to be "canonical." All of the books which were thus accepted as "canonical" comprised the Old Testament. Thus it came about that the list of books in the Old Testament —thirty-nine in all, was known as the Canon. And so we speak of the Canon of the Old Testament, by which we mean the thirty-nine books that were accepted as authoritative.

2. *The Canon of the English and the Hebrew Bibles.* The original Hebrew Canon contained only twenty-four books in contrast with thirty-nine which we have in our printed English Bible. This was due to the Hebrews' combining books that were listed separately in the English Bible, thereby reducing the number of books. But the Hebrew Canon and the English Canon contained identically the same books. As indicated in an earlier section, the early Hebrew Canon was divided into three parts as follows:

LAW _____ 5
　　　Genesis, Exodus, Leviticus, Numbers, Deuteronomy

PROPHETS (divided into two groups) _____ 8

Former Prophets _____ 4
　　Joshua　　Samuel (1 and 2)
　　Judges　　Kings (1 and 2)

Latter Prophets _____ 4
　　Isaiah　　　Ezekiel

Jeremiah   Book of the Twelve
                (included all 12 minor
                prophets)

THE WRITINGS _____ 11
        (In Hebrew, *Kethubhim;* in Greek, *Hagiography*)

Poetical Books _____ 3
        Psalms, Proverbs, Job

The Five Rolls (Megilloth) _____ 5
        Song of Solomon   Ecclesiastes
        Ruth   Esther
        Lamentations

Historical Books _____ 3
        Daniel
        Ezra-Nehemiah (combined as one book)
        Chronicles (1 and 2 as one book)

Total Number of Books   24

It was from this threefold canon that Jesus and the early apostles quoted, and to which reference is made in the books of the New Testament. Various opinions have been expressed in an effort to explain the reason for this threefold division. One view is that they reveal the three stages by which the Old Testament books were given canonical recognition. That is, the Pentateuch was first accepted as canonical, then at a later time the Prophets, and last of all the Writings.

3. *Historical Confirmation of the Canon.* Space does not permit consideration of the large amount of data showing the gradual process by which the Canon was developed, and the confirmation of the thirty-nine books as authoritative for the Jewish faith. Reference books listed at the end of the chapter will supply that detailed information.

When the destruction of Jerusalem in A.D. 70 seemed imminent, permission was secured from the Romans by the Rabbi Yochanan ben Zakkai to set up the Jewish Sanhedrin on a purely spiritual basis at Jabneh or Jamnia. The city of Jamnia was located between Joppa and

Azotus (Ashdod). At Jamnia debates of many kinds were carried on by the Sanhedrin. One of these debates concerned the question of whether certain books should or should not be included in the Hebrew Canon. Objections had been raised against such books as the Book of Esther, which did not contain the name of God. The conclusions reached at Jamnia, at the council held there in A.D. 90-100, confirmed the thirty-nine books now contained in both the Hebrew and the Protestant Old Testament canons.

Scholars have noted that Jamnia was not an official council. Perhaps what should be pointed out is the fact that Jamnia simply confirmed the already existing conviction of the Jewish people; it did not form or create that conviction. In other words, the thirty-nine books "had already been established in the hearts of the faithful with an authority that could not be shaken nor confirmed by the decisions of the schools."[2]

4. *The Basis of Selection.* There would seem to be two tests to apply to each book to determine its admission to the Canon. The first would be whether the book was in harmony with the main purpose of God's revelation of himself. Perhaps this could best be illustrated from the New Testament. A book to be admitted into the New Testament canon had to be faithful to the Event—the life, death and resurrection of Jesus. Similarly, a book to be admitted to the Old Testament canon must be faithful to the event—the great act of God in bringing into existence the covenant community of Israel through which his revelation was to be given. That event was the Exodus and those other events related to it.

The second test was whether the book had a direct historical connection with the revelation of God in history. "If the book gives us a link in the history of that revelation, or if it represents a stage of God's dealings,

[2]Marcus Dods, *The Bible, Its Origin and Nature*, p. 54.

and if it contains nothing which is quite inconsistent with the idea of being inspired, then its claim to be admitted seems valid."[3] Thus, the first five books of the Old Testament, the Pentateuch, are in harmony with each other, and each has a direct historical connection with the revelation of God as it was given in the great historic event of the Exodus, the giving of the Law at Sinai, and the events which followed. The same thing is true of the books of history, prophecy, and the other writings.

SECTION 4. THE INSPIRATION OF THE OLD TESTAMENT

A study of this kind often leads to many questions about the inspiration of the Old Testament. These introductory sections have already indicated that there was a human aspect involved in the preparation of the Old Testament. As the study proceeds the human element involved in the writing of these books will become more evident. Students of the Old Testament are generally agreed that there were both divine and human factors working together to produce the Scriptures.

1. *Relation of the Human and the Divine Aspects.* The following statement will serve to introduce the relation of these two factors in the production of the Old Testament:

That the Scriptures are divinely given is shown by such texts as 2 Timothy 3:16 and 2 Peter 1:21. That they were written by men is equally clear from many texts, such as John 1:17; Romans 1:1; Galatians 6:11. God adapted his truth to ordinary human intelligence by shaping it in human molds. The Scriptures are a result of the interworking of the human and divine, not of one without the other. This divine inspiration of the sacred writers was not an external force, acting upon them from without; but was from within and through their natural faculties, intellect, and personality. From what we can gather from the scriptural teaching and from personal experience today as to the manner of the working of God's Spirit, we

[3]*Ibid.,* p. 54.

are safe in believing that these writers retained full use of every human faculty, but that the Holy Spirit exalted the exercise of those natural powers.[4]

It is evident from the study of the Scriptures that the writers of the several books were not mere machines or scribes, who wrote as God dictated, nor were their personalities suppressed when they were illuminated or inspired by the Holy Spirit. Neither were their powers of memory and imagination, understanding and judgment, and will inactive while under the inspiration of the Holy Spirit. That this is true will be seen from the following examples:

(1) *The Use of Source Materials.* Quotations in some of the books of the Old Testament have been taken from older books and writings which have disappeared. Numbers 21:14f. is quoted from the "Book of the Wars of Yahweh"; while Joshua 10:12f., 2 Samuel 1:19-27, and 1 Kings 8:12f. are said to be taken from the Book of Jasher. The author of the Book of Chronicles makes reference to ten books which have disappeared, but which were doubtless used as source material. Court records were also used in the writing of the Books of Kings. In the New Testament Luke (1:1-4) gives us a picture of himself using a number of already existing accounts of the life and ministry of Jesus in writing his Gospel.

(2) *The Inclusion of Personal Experiences.* In the Psalms reference is made to personal experiences in many areas of life and religion. These are told to point out God's mighty deliverance, or his gift of forgiveness, or his providential care. The personal experiences of Moses, as given in the first and last parts of Deuteronomy is another example of this personal human element found in the Scriptures.

(3) *A Difference in Literary Style.* In the second

[4]Russell R. Byrum, *Christian Theology* (3rd ed.; Gospel Trumpet Co., 1950), pp. 171-172.

part of Isaiah (chaps. 40-66) there are passages of ex-
quisite beauty, poetic in form, which stand out in contrast with the ordinary prose of the Books of Kings and
Chronicles. The writer of those last chapters of Isaiah
has been called the Milton of Hebrew poetry, and one
author speaks of him as "supreme and unrivalled
among the great poets of the world."[5] And throughout
the entire thirty-nine books of the Old Testament we
find this difference of literary style. Such contrasts in
style are also noted throughout the New Testament.

The conclusion drawn from these few examples is
that the Holy Spirit used the writers of the Old Testament without destroying their individuality and sup-
pressing their personalities. Their personal differences,
their peculiar talents and education, their likes and dis-
likes came to view in the books they have written. Yet,
while the Bible is a book that has come through the in-
strumentality of man, and every book bears the mark
of human authorship, it is at the same time a book that
comes from God and was written under the inspiration
of the Holy Spirit.

2. *Revelation and Inspiration.* A better understanding of this subject will be obtained if we consider
the idea of "revelation" along with the idea of "inspiration," for an understanding of both is necessary to
appreciate God's part in giving us the Scriptures.

(1) *The meaning of Revelation.* The purpose of divine revelation is the disclosure of God to man. This is
spoken of as the divine self-disclosure. That disclosure
makes known something of the nature of God as well
as the will and purpose of God for mankind.

The word "revelation" means to unveil or uncover.
As the veil is pulled aside, something that was hidden is
disclosed or brought to view. And this is the whole idea
of revelation in the Scriptures. Something that was hidden has now been revealed or disclosed.

[5] C. C. Tory, *The Second Isaiah*, p. 91.

It is quite usual for people to think of this revelation or this disclousre as consisting of a body of information about God, his nature and ethical characteristics, his will and his purpose for mankind and the world. But the essential meaning of revelation is not that of God communicating a body of information to us through the prophets and through his apostles, but rather that of God unveiling himself and disclosing himself to men. In that act or in those acts of unveiling and making himself known, prophets and apostles of old came to understand something of the nature and character of God, as well as his will and purpose for men. Revelation is not a timeless communication of ideas from God, but an account of what happened. In the words of John Baillie: "God reveals himself in *action*—in the gracious activity by which he invades the field of human experience and human history which is otherwise but a vain show, empty and drained of meaning."[6] This self-disclosure of God reaches its highest when God himself becomes incarnate in Jesus Christ.

(2) *God Reveals Himself in Action.* The God of the Old Testament is the God of history. He makes himself known in a series of events in which he showed himself in his work, carrying out his purpose and revealing his nature by what he did. The Old Testament covers a long period of history, a period sufficiently long to reveal the broad outlines of God's will and purpose for men. The Scriptures are essentially the story of the acts of God. Go through your Old Testament and note those events. G. Ernest Wright[7] lists five events in which he considers the whole faith of Israel to be centered. They are: (1) The call of the Israelite patriarchs and the promises God made to them; (2) the Exodus from Egypt; (3) the covenant made with Israel at Sinai; (4)

---

[6]John Baillie, *The Idea of Revelation in Recent Thought* (Columbia University Press, 1956), p. 49.
[7]G. Ernest Wright and Reginald H. Fuller, *The Book of the Acts of God* (Doubleday, 1957), pp. 18-22.

the conquest of Canaan; and (5) the Davidic kingdom and government. Some feel that there are other events that should be included, such as God's actions in connection with the Assyrian and Babylonian threats to the Israelites, the Captivity and Exile, the return from Babylon, the restoration and the rebuilding of the Temple. The prophets were men who were intensely conscious of these great historical events being the mighty acts of God.

In the New Testament we see this idea of God revealing himself through events more clearly defined. The Incarnation, through which God discloses himself in Jesus Christ, the death and resurrection of Jesus, the descent of the Holy Spirit, and events which followed reveal to us something of the nature and character of God, his salvation, and his purposes for men.

(3) *These Events Must Be Interpreted.* The event, whether in the Old Testament or in the New Testament, would not be revelation, that is, would not reveal anything, unless it were understood. This means that what happened must be interpreted. It is only as the activities of God in history—in the Old and New Testaments—are understood as God means them to be understood that there is a revelation of God and his purpose. There must be a "receiving" on the part of man as well as a "giving" on the part of God.

This means that the mind of man, who is the receiver of the revelation, must be illuminated to receive or understand what God is trying to disclose in the event. Dr. William Temple states that this whole process is guided by God. The event takes place and the mind of the prophet is guided by God so that he comes to understand the meaning of that event as God would have him understand it. Let us think of this with respect to the coming of Christ and his work of redemption. The birth of Jesus Christ into our world and his living and teaching among men is not revelation if he is not recognized by anybody as the Christ, the Son of the living

God. Likewise, his death and resurrection are not revelations of God's redeeming purpose unless somebody
understands the meaning of that death and resurrection
and finds redemption through trusting in the God who
gave his Son to die for man. Both prophets and apostles believed that it was only through the illumination
that came from God that they were able to interpret or
understand the mighty acts of God. The words of
Amos are in accord with this belief: "Surely the Lord
God does nothing, without revealing his secret to his
servants the prophets" (Amos 3:7). This illumination
is what is meant by inspiration. It was a very necessary
part of the revelation. "No prophecy ever originated in
the human will, but under the influence of the Holy
Spirit men spoke for God" (2 Pet. 1:21).[8]

(4) *The Written Witness*. After the illumination had
come to the prophet or the apostle under the influence
of the Holy Spirit, he then gave witness or testified to
what God had revealed to him. At first this was an oral
or spoken witness, as was the case with the prophets
and with the apostles who had kept company with
Jesus and were eyewitnesses of those great events associated with the life, death, and resurrection of Jesus.
But here we are mainly concerned with the written witness or testimony. The Bible, then, is the written witness of what the prophets and apostles, through the illumination given to them by God through his Holy
Spirit, understood to be what had been revealed. Thus,
by a sovereign act God selected Israel and led her people out of Egypt. Then it was given to Moses and to
the prophets that followed him, to understand the significance and meaning of that basic event in the Old
Testament. God so loved the world that he gave his
Son to die for men. At the same time there was given
to his apostles that illumination which enabled them to

[8] J. M. Powis Smith and Edgar J. Goodspeed (translators), *The
Complete Bible, An American Translation* (University of Chicago
Press, 1939).

grasp the meaning of that great event. To that event the apostles gave witness, at first orally, and then in the written documents that now comprise our New Testament.

The witness, both spoken and written, was a human activity, as was pointed out in the beginning of this section. "Nevertheless, we cannot believe that God, having performed his mighty acts and having illumined the minds of prophet and apostle to understand their true import, left the prophetic and apostolic *testimony* to take care of itself. It were indeed a strange conception of divine providential activity which would deny that the biblical writers were divinely assisted in their attempt to communicate to the world the illumination which for the world's sake they had themselves received. The same Holy Spirit who had enlightened them unto their own salvation must also have aided their efforts, whether spoken or written, to convey the message of salvation to those whom their words would reach. This is what is meant by the inspiration of the Holy Scripture."[9]

This emphasis upon God's revelation in history is not meant to rule out the clear scriptural fact that God communicated freely with man in order to reveal his will. The experience of Moses at the burning bush is an example. In that experience God communicated directly to Moses, making known his purposes and intentions for the people of Israel.

(5) *Through the Bible God Now Reveals Himself.* If one is to know God [for himself], God must reveal himself. Such a knowledge of God must be a fact of one's own personal experience. But how does one come to have such a personal knowledge of God? It comes through the written witness or testimony—the Bible. Through the written testimony of the past, which we

have in the Scriptures, God reveals himself to man in the present.

Had there been no contemporary prophetic interpretation of God's dealings with Israel, and no contemporary apostolic interpretation of the Gospel history, I could not at this distance be finding the presence of God in them at all. It is probable that I would never have heard about them, and certain that I would never have understood them. On the other hand, I could not know that God had revealed himself to the prophets and apostles through these events, unless through his revelation of himself to them he were now revealing himself to me. I could know indeed that they claimed to have received such a revelation, but I can know that their claim was justified only if, as I read what they say, I too find myself in the presence of God.[10]

SUGGESTIONS FOR FURTHER STUDY ON CHAPTER I

General Background

Anderson, Bernhard, *Understanding the Old Testament* (Prentice-Hall, 1957); pages 1-10.

Flanders, Crapps and Smith, *People of the Covenant* (The Ronald Press, 1963); chapter I.

Robinson, H. Wheeler, *The Old Testament, Its Making and Meaning* (Cokesbury, 1937); chapters I and II.

Wright, G. Ernest and Fuller, Reginald H., *The Book of the Acts of God* (Doubleday, 1957); chapter I.

Canon and Text

Barclay, William, *The Making of the Bible* (Abingdon, 1961).

Bruce, F. F., *The Books and the Parchments* (Pickering, 1950).

Filson, Floyd V., *Which Books Belong in the Bible* (Westminster, 1957).

Kenyon, Frederick, *Our Bible and the Ancient Manuscripts* (Harper, 1958).

Revelation and Inspiration

Baillie, John, *The Idea of Revelation in Recent Thought* (Columbia University Press, 1956).

Berkhof, L., *Principles of Bible Interpretation* (Baker, 1950); chapter IV.

Snaith, Norman, *The Inspiration and Authority of the Bible* (Epworth, 1956).

[10]*Ibid.*, p. 105.

PART I: THE PENTATEUCH AND JOSHUA

CHAPTER II

THE BOOKS OF GENESIS AND EXODUS

(The Early Beginnings of Israel: Part I)

We have already reviewed the Old Testament story in very brief form in chapter 1. We come now to consider that story in more detail by looking at each of the thirty-nine books, noting how each is related to "the historical action of God seeking the reconciliation of man and God."

Seventeen of these books give us the broad outlines of Israel's history. They are the books listed in our English Bible from Genesis to and including Esther. The accounts they give are by no means continuous or a complete chronological narrative such as we would expect to find in textbooks of history today. They do give us, however, the great events of Hebrew history. In addition we have the historical data found in the other books of the Old Testament, especially in the Prophets. To these sources must be added the mass of information which archaeologists are continually making available. When all of these are taken together, it is possible to see clearly the history of the chosen people as it reveals God's purpose both for them and for the whole world.

Perhaps here is the place to call attention to the fact that these seventeen books are usually divided into two groups. Group I is made up of those books from Genesis to Kings. Group II includes Chronicles, Ezra, and

Nehemiah. The first group of books begins with the story of creation and carries the account down to the time of the Exile. The second group begins with Adam and tells the story down to the period of Ezra and Nehemiah after the Exile.

In these two accounts there are duplications and parallel accounts. The story given in the second group is mainly concerned with Israel's history as related to the Temple and the priesthood. (A fuller discussion is found in chapter 9). The Book of Ruth, included in the first group, is a story whose background is that of early Hebrew history, while Esther relates to events in the very late period of that history.

SECTION 1. THE PENTATEUCH

In the next two chapters we shall study the five books which comprise the Pentateuch, along with a sixth one—the Book of Joshua, which completes the study of the early beginnings of Israel.

1. *The Origin of the Pentateuch.* In the former chapter reference was made to the stages of development in the literature of the Old Testament; the oral stage, the stage in which fragmentary or partial accounts appeared, and finally the stage of completed books. Since no attempt was made to explain how all this came about, a brief consideration should be given to the theories of composition of these first five books of the Old Testament. A great deal of discussion revolves around the divergent points of view regarding the authorship and composition of the Pentateuch. Space does not permit detailed discussion of this matter, but the following brief summarization of two widely divergent points of view will serve to introduce the topic.

(1) *The Traditional Approach.* This approach insists upon the Mosaic authorship of these books. Two quotations from exponents of this view will be suffi-

cient. This view is often called the "Conservative Theory." Unger quotes Professor Dick Wilson as expressing this point of view:

That the Pentateuch as it stands is historical and from the time of Moses; and that Moses was its real author, though it may have been revised and edited by later redactors, the additions being just as inspired as the rest.[1]

Edward J. Young, a leading spokesman for the Conservative conclusion today is in agreement with Professor Wilson's statement:

The witness of sacred Scripture leads us to believe that Moses was the *fundamental* or *real* author of the Pentateuch. In composing it, he may indeed, as Astruc suggested, have employed parts of previously existing documents. Also, under Divine Inspiration, there may have been later minor additions and revisions. Substantially and essentially, however, it is the product of Moses.[2]

This theory does not preclude "later redactions of the whole work and to allow that, during the course of the centuries of the transmission of the text, certain modifications were introduced into the work, such as additions after the death of Moses, modernization of archaic expressions and place names, marginal glosses or explanatory scribal insertions, which eventually crept into the text, and textual errors due to inadvertent mistakes of copyists." However, this point of view holds that substantially in form and extent the Pentateuch as we have it now dates from the time of Moses.

(2) *The Documentary Theory.* This view of the origin of the Pentateuch suggests there are four basic sources, which are designated J, E, D, and P. The J source, also known as the Yahwist source because it gives prominence to Yahweh as the name for God, is

---

[1] Merrill F. Unger, *Introductory Guide to the Old Testament* (Zondervan, 1952), p. 237.

[2] Edward J. Young, *An Introduction to the Old Testament* (Eerdmans, 1949), p. 51.

said to be the earliest source and is usually dated about 950 B.C. during the early years of the monarchy.

The E source, also designated as Elohist because it uses Elohim as the name for God, is dated in either the ninth or eighth century B.C. The D source reflects the teachings of the Book of Deuteronomy and is dated about 650 B.C. The fourth source or P is dated during the Exile (after 587 B.C.), and is attributed to a circle of priests who had saved some of the records from the archives of the Temple before it·was destroyed. This theory holds that these sources were woven together in various stages at different times, and that our present Pentateuch represents a composite of these sources, completed about 400 B.C.

(3) *Present-day Trends*. Trends in Old Testament scholarship today may be summed up as follows:

　　a) A recognition that the material which comes from the earliest life of Israel as a people (tenth century and before) "is by no means inconsiderable in bulk."[3] John Bright further states that the Decalogue in its original form is Mosaic, and that the Book of the Covenant (Exod. 21-23), instead of being dated in the ninth century, is of very early origin, with much of it belonging to the generation of Moses.

On the basis of the above and similar statements by other scholars, it can be believed that before Moses' death he left a record of the significant events with which he had been associated. Whether this record was written or in oral form we have no way of knowing now, but it seems certain that the contribution of Moses became the nucleus of what we know now as the Pentateuch. If Moses is to be considered the author of the Pentateuch, it is not in the sense that he wrote it in its entirety, not word for word, or even book for book. A study of the Pentateuch reveals the fact that the style, syntax, and vocabulary differ a great deal in dif-

[3]John Bright, *A History of Israel* (Westminster, 1959), p. 150.

ferent sections of the books, testifying to the existence of parallel sources. As a result the Pentateuch is believed to be the result of a long literary process begun and inspired by Moses and continued in his spirit.

b) It is recognized today that there was a long period of oral transmission before the preparation of the earliest written account of the central fact of the Pentateuch—the Exodus. One writer suggests that this oral period was more than three hundred years. During this period the material was transmitted from father to son to grandson with a high degree of accuracy. In this way the record was preserved, passed on, and later collected to be written down when the developments within Israel required it.

Peoples in the days of Israel's beginning did not give the significance to writing we do today. For the most part writing was confined to specialists. The people "learned by heart" the things that were most important. It is said that the people of the Near East still retain this skill, and that some Arabs can recite the entire Koran without a mistake, even though they can neither read nor write.

This transmission by word of mouth of such important material was facilitated by the fact that the various events and specific acts constituted, or were in the form of, what we call "memory units." There were certain characteristics of these units that aided in memorizing, such as "a monotonous but smooth-flowing style, recurrent expressions, and a certain rhythm and euphony." One example of such memory units is found in Deuteronomy 26:5-10. In this manner the great stories and accounts in Genesis and Exodus were handed down.

c) It should be remembered that along with the materials that were transmitted orally, there were other materials, such as those noted under *a* (page 31) which were handed down in written form. Thus the oral and

the written materials became the basis of our completed Pentateuch as we have it today.

(4) *The Pentateuch as a Single Book.* The Pentateuch was conceived as a single book and one will understand and appreciate its message only if he sees and
interprets each of its five parts in relation to the whole
document. Thus Genesis accounts for the origin of the
chosen people of God; Exodus explains how Israel
emerged as a distinct people through the Exodus and at
Sinai; Leviticus makes clear that this nation is to be a
holy nation; Numbers outlines the organizational structure of the community of God; Deuteronomy sets forth
love as the basis of relationship to God and to each
other in this chosen community.

SECTION 2. THE BOOK OF GENESIS

The Book of Genesis is great literature. Measured by
the standards of literary excellence it is given a high
place among the great works of human literature. Luther's estimate was that "nothing is more beautiful than
Genesis, nothing more useful." But Genesis is more than
great literature. It is an account of God's revelation of
himself as Creator and Savior. It is more than human
writing, for behind it all and through it breathes the
Holy Spirit whose presence is the very inspiration of
the book.

1. *The Title.* The title of this first book comes from
the Septuagint or Greek translation where 2:4 reads:
"This is the book of *geneseōs* of heaven and earth."
When the Latin Vulgate translation was made the title
"Genesis," taken from the Latin, was used to designate
this first book. The word means becoming or beginning, and is a translation from the first word of the Hebrew text of Genesis, *B'reshith,* which means "in the
beginning." In the Hebrew Old Testament all of the
books were designated by the opening words of the
books. Since this title means origin, source, generation,

it has been used by nearly all translations as the name of the book. It well indicates the contents as well as the purpose of the writer.

2. *Theme and Purpose.* The theme is the origin of the chosen or covenant people of God—Israel. The purpose is to show how God prepared the Hebrew people to be his chosen nation. One writer sees behind the Genesis document "Israel's consciousness of standing in a unique relationship to God, the Creator, the controller of history, the source of all righteousness, the foundation of all meaning. The purpose of the book is to account for this sense of uniqueness, to establish its validity, and to show that it originated not in what today would be called wishful thinking, but in God's free act of choice."[4]

H. A. Alleman defines this purpose as follows: "The writer of Genesis had a definite plan. He set himself the task of preserving not the story of human history but the story of salvation. To this end he must needs tell the story of the beginnings of life, of man, of sin, of hope, of faith, while back of all stood his God who was without beginning and by whose words all things come to be. . . . The [the Hebrews] had a great and unique experience, and they cherished the sense of mission in the world which their God had inspired in them. All the books of the Old Testament breathe this consciousness. The writer of Genesis had the profoundest sense of it. His purpose was to tell how Jehovah had singled his people out from all the peoples of the world to have this experience, and to tell what their God had revealed himself to be and what he had made of them."[5]

The purpose of the writer becomes clearer as one notes how he develops the book. It is usual to divide the book into two parts as follows:

Part I. *The beginnings of the world and of man*

[4]*The Interpreter's Bible,* "purpose" by Cuthbert A. Simpson, I, 440.
[5]*Lutheran Commentary,* p. 171.

(1:1—11:9) Chapters 1—2 set forth some basic truths about God and man. In the rest of this first part the emphasis is on the failure to preserve the knowledge of God universally, due to a disruption in man's relationship with God. The failure is well marked for that period before the Flood, since the Flood is the culmination of man's evil and wickedness. The progressive deterioration of mankind underscores the need for active participation on the part of God if man is to truly conquer the forces of evil.

Part II. *The beginnings of the Hebrew nation* (11:10—50:26). The revelation of God is now directed toward the preparation of a chosen family set apart from the pagan world and eventually to bring salvation to that world. That was the family of the Mesopotamian patriarch Abraham, from whom descended Isaac and Jacob and the twelve tribes of Israel. The descendants of Jacob settle in Egypt, and at the critical moment they are ready to be welded into God's chosen nation.

The Book of Genesis records the early stages of God's revelation, which was to unfold and become clearer in the centuries following the selection of Abraham. With the coming of Christ in the "fullness of time," the revelation moves out into all the world in its universal appeal.

3. *Contents of Genesis.* The following brief outline will point out the main contents of the book:

1. The Prologue: Primeval or Prehistory of the World and Mankind (chaps. 1:1—11:9).

2. The History of Abraham (chaps. 11:10—24:67).

3. The History of Isaac and Jacob (chaps. 25—36).

4. The History of Joseph in Egypt (chaps. 37—50).

There are some significant passages which highlight

the teachings or theology of the Book of Genesis that should be noted here.

(1) *The Creation* (1:1—2:25). The inspired author's purpose is to teach religion and not science. In other words, he is interested in the "what" and "why" of things, not the "how." Nothing is said as to how it was done, that is, about process. "Science is concerned with material and phenomenal things, with processes and changes, with differentiation and combination. This account does not deny the process; it ignores it. It speaks in terms of divine fiat, which can both use and dispense with process. Science deals with second causes: here the First Cause is the Almighty Actor, and second causes are ignored."[6]

Anderson is of the opinion that "the stories concerning primeval history cannot be regarded as exact, factual accounts of the sort that the modern historian or scientist demands. These stories are 'historical' only in the sense that, as used by the Yahwist (the author), they communicate the *meaning of history*. The manner of presentation is pictorial, for the writer is dealing with a subject that eludes the modern historian's investigation—namely, the ultimate source of the human drama in the purpose and activity of God."[7]

Such a view as that expressed by Anderson focuses attention upon God as Creator, the source and ground of all being, that man is creature and dependent upon God, and that God had and does have a purpose for man and the world.

A. F. Gray, who presents a conservative position, stresses the historical value of the creation accounts in Genesis.

[6]Oswald T. Allis, *God Spake by Moses* (Presbyterian and Reformed, 1951), p. 10.

[7]Bernhard W. Anderson, *Understanding the Old Testament* (Prentice-Hall, 1957), p. 167.

Accepting the poetic nature of the first account of creation does not destroy its historic value. The language is in some measure figurative and yet true. An American poet wrote "The poorest twig on the elm tree is ridged inch deep with pearl." This was not literally true but was poetic description of a fact—the sparkling white snow on the tree. The fact that the description is poetic does not require us to deny the existence of the tree. And so in the Genesis account, though we recognize its poetic nature we should still regard it as substantially historical.[8]

Cartledge summarizes the conservative viewpoint as follows:

It is possible to point to Babylonian parallels to the stories of Creation and of the Flood. Some say that that proves that the biblical accounts were simply legends like those, or even were derived from those. No one can ascertain the origin of those primitive records in the Bible. Some feel that they may have come from a special revelation from God, while others feel that they may contain much legendary matter. Even if the latter be true, the striking thing is the way the Bible used them to teach the wonderful religious truths.[9]

(2) *The Beginnings of Sin* (3:1-24). The account here underscores sin as an act of the will in which man revolts against God. Man wants to step out of his position as man and be "like God." The principal story of the creation of man is on his *creaturehood*. He is made from the dust of the ground and is to return to the ground. But he is more than animal; he is the creature God made by breathing into him the breath of life so that "man became a living soul." This means that man's existence in this world is related to God and is dependent upon him. Man is free, as God speaks to him, to obey or disobey. Having disobeyed God, all the tragic results of that sin followed. Revolt against God brings man the judgment of God. That judgment was that man would live his life in suffering and anxiety, with the threat of death hanging over his head. This

[8]A. F. Gray, *Studies in Christian Doctrine*, Vol. I.
[9]Samuel Cartledge, *A Conservative Introduction to the Old Testament* (Zondervan Publishing House, 1948), p. 66.

judgment is overcome through the redemptive work of Christ.

(3) *The Beginnings of Society* (4:1—11:9). The story of Cain and Abel is designed to show that as a result of the revolt of Adam against God, evil followed in its train. Family life was broken up and the community life in the process of becoming was disrupted by Cain being forced to flee. The story of the intermarriage of the sons of God (not heavenly beings, but those who were not in open revolt against God) with the daughters of men (those living in open revolt against God) is designed to show that ultimately the distinction between the two lines was lost, and the result was that "the wickedness of man was great in the earth, and that every imagination of the thoughts of his heart was only evil continually" (Gen. 6:5).

The Flood which followed is described by the writer as the judgment of God. It reflects the view of the Hebrews that God's judgment is seen in the events of history. But God's judgment is always related to man's redemption. He has concern and care for man. A remnant is preserved, Noah and his family, and from them there is to be a new beginning in man's history. After the judgment comes the promise that such a judgment would not fall upon the earth again.

The story of *the new beginning* points out that the judgment of God did not purge the evil from the heart of man. It tells how the evil of men's hearts became more evident. Noah's intoxication and the implied sexual abomination, and the story of the Tower of Babel illustrates man's condition. Man's desire to assert himself—to step out of his position of being dependent upon God as his creature and be as God—again manifests itself. The Tower of Babel becomes the symbol of mankind's united effort to proclaim their independence of God. If they could build the tower to reach to heaven, they could exercise the same authority that God exercised. The story reveals man's desire for greatness and power. He hoped to achieve this by bringing all of the communities together in unity and close cooperation. When that was achieved they would express their total independence of God. The story then describes the judgment and the dispersion of the various language groups throughout the world.

The conclusion drawn from the study of these first eleven chapters is that man failed to experience what had been God's purpose for him, namely fellowship with God and with his fellowmen within established communities. These chapters also reveal considerable development and achievement in the arts of civilization; yet, in spite of such progress and advancement, evil continued to increase. It was this evil which led to man's estrangement from God and necessitated the next step, which may be called the first step in the redemption of man, God's selection of Abraham as the father of the Hebrew nation.

(4) *The History of Abraham, Isaac, Jacob, and Joseph* (11:10—50:26). The histories of Abraham, Isaac, Jacob, and Joseph are important because they form an introduction to the central theme in the entire Old Testament record, namely the unique place of Israel in God's purpose to bring about the redemption of mankind.

Before looking at the biblical account, mention should be made of the general confirmation which archaeological discoveries have given to the accounts of Abraham's life as given in the Book of Genesis. Until these discoveries were made the old critical theory held that the stories in Genesis were artificial narratives composed late in the history of Israel. It is now known that in the Genesis records which concern Abraham and his family "we are here dealing with genuine society of the early part of the second millennium B.C."[10] This is supported by W. F. Albright:

[10] J. A. Thompson, *The Bible and Archaeology* (Eerdmans, 1962), p. 26.

So many corroborations of details have been discovered in recent years that most competent scholars have given up the old critical theory according to which the stories of the patriarchs are mostly retrojections from the time of the dual monarchy, 9th-8th centuries B.C.[11]

The Book of Genesis places the home of Abraham in or near the city of Ur in the lower part of Mesopotamia. This was part of that area known as the Fertile Crescent. A Bible atlas will outline this area for you as a crescent-shaped strip of land starting at the Persian Gulf and bending around the northern tip of the Arabian desert, then curving down around Syria and Palestine, and continuing toward the Nile river in Egypt. This area was the cradle of civilization and archaeologists have given biblical students and the world a wealth of information concerning the development of that civilization for centuries before the first Hebrews came upon the scene of action.

A precise date for Abraham and the patriarchs who followed cannot be determined, but it is generally agreed that they should be placed in the period from 200—1700 B.C., perhaps earlier in that period rather than later. The importance of Ur during the centuries preceding Abraham is readily seen in the archaeological discoveries. Excavations have revealed something of the splendor of that important city. Thompson writes of that period as follows:

The royal tombs of Ur, dating to about 2500 B.C., produced a collection of magnificent golden vessels which are still the delight and wonderment of students of the ancient world. Ur was a town with a complex system of government and a well-developed system of commerce, one with writing in common use for the issue of receipts, the making of contracts, and many other purposes. There were town drains, streets, two-storied houses, a great temple tower (ziggurat), trade routes joining the town with other

[11]W. F. Albright, *Archaeology and the Religion of Israel* (2nd ptg., Johns Hopkins, 1941), p. 183.

great towns to the north and south, and various other evidences of a highly developed civilization.[12]

The history of Abraham is related to the peoples who lived in Mesopotamia before him as well as during his period and that which followed. The first settlers in that area were the Sumerians. Very early, Semitic peoples began to enter this region. They were known as the Akkadians. They displaced the Sumerians and took over their culture. Later, other Semitic peoples, the Amorites and the Aramaeans, came into these areas. All of this is good evidence for the Genesis account that Abraham came out of Ur of the Chaldees though we cannot be certain about which group of Semites it was from which Abraham's family came.

Since space does not permit any extensive discussion of the various peoples whose life and activities constitute the background of this period, the following summary will be helpful in understanding the importance of both the times and the region around the time of the patriarchs.

a) *Sumerians and Akkadians.* 3000—2000 B.C. See explanation above.

b) *The Amorites.* These are Semites who moved from the Arabian desert into lower Mesopotamia about 2000 B.C. By 1800—1750 B.C. all of Mesopotamia was under the control of the Amorites. Hammurabi belongs to this period.

c) *The Hurrian Movement.* These people are called Horites in the Old Testament, and their movement started about 2000 B.C. By 1500 B.C. they controlled the important Mesopotamian state of Mitannu. Nuzu, an important town east of the Tigris river, yielded important information in the form of clay tablets or documents when excavated in recent years. The customs of the people were quite similar to those of the patriarchs.

[12]Thompson, *op. cit.*, pp. 16-17.

d) *The Hittites.* 1600—1500 B.C. It is believed
these people originated somewhere in Europe and constituted part of the great Indo-European migration
which reached as far as India. The group of Hittites of
interest to us here is that which settled in the area we
now know as Turkey. They moved into Mesopotamia,
and Genesis 23 states that Abraham purchased a burial
site from them.

It is thought that Abraham's migration from Haran
in Mesopotamia to Canaan took place at the time of
the Amorite invasion of Mesopotamia and Syria. Before Abraham received his call from God, his father
Terah had moved to Haran. It was after the death of
his father in Haran that Abraham received his call to
leave Mesopotamia. Haran was an Amorite settlement
at the time, which lends support to the view that Abraham's departure from Canaan was related to the military and political developments in that region.

(5) *The Selection of Abraham.* From among the Semitic peoples of Mesopotamia, God selected one man
with which to start the unfolding of his great purpose
of redemption. This is the promise he made to Abraham: "I will make of you a great nation, and I will
bless you, . . . and by you all the families of the earth
will bless themselves" (Gen. 12:2-3). The promise
was threefold:

a) that he would possess a land
b) that he would become a great nation
c) that he would be a blessing to all peoples.

This, then, is the beginning of a new kind of history,
called sacred history by some, but by whatever name it
is called it is the beginning of a history in which is unfolded the action of Yahweh in a single family at first
—Abraham, Isaac, Jacob, and Joseph, and then
through the nation of Israel in order that the blessing of
redemption might come to all men.

The history of this family, bound together by the tie
of father and son, need not be noted in detail here. The

Book of Genesis ends with the account of Joseph's rise
to prominence as prime minister of Egypt, the migration of Jacob's family to Egypt as a result of the famine, and a general picture of contentment and security
while Joseph and the Israelites remained in favor with
the pharaohs.

The Book of Exodus then resumes the story, but at a
point where the fortunes of the Israelites have changed,
for a new dynasty of rulers now governs Egypt. The
following outline will fill in the events connected with
the history of the patriarchs.

OUTLINE OF CHAPTERS 11:10 to 50:26 OF GENESIS

(Beginnings of the Hebrew Nation)

SECTION 3. THE BOOK OF EXODUS

"The Book of Exodus," says J. C. Rylaarsdam, "is comparable to a drama. The action consists of God's preparation for the deliverance of the enslaved Hebrews, his victory over Pharaoh, which accomplishes their rescue, and his establishment of Israel as his people. The action and triumph of God is the center from which the whole book proceeds."[13] While the entire Pentateuch is concerned with the account of the unfolding of God's purpose of redemption for man, the Book of Exodus is especially concerned with the central fact of that story—the emergence of Israel as God's chosen people and the events which led up to that unique happening.

1. *General Background.* The Book of Genesis closed with Joseph, Jacob, and his family settling in Egypt and enjoying the favor and goodwill of the Egyptian rulers. With the opening of the Book of Exodus we find the situation has changed, for a "king arose who knew not Joseph," and the settlement of Israelites were subject to severe ill-treatment.

(1) *The Hyksos Dynasty's Occupation of Egypt and Canaan.* The movement of the Hebrew people into Egypt began about 1700 B.C. Just prior to the descent of the Hebrews into Egypt, Canaan and Egypt were invaded by a group of people who later became known as the Hyksos, or "rulers of foreign countries." They overthrew the native Egyptian dynasty about 1710 B.C. and built an empire of their own, which included Palestine. Since the Hyksos rulers of Egypt were Semites, the migration of the Hebrews to Egypt and their pros-

---

[13] *The Interpreter's Bible,* I, p. 833.

perity there were facilitated by having a favorable dynasty in control. This was a time when conditions were right for Joseph to hold the position of prime minister in Pharaoh's court.

A revolution in Egypt in 1570 B.C. drove the Hyksos out of Egypt and the Israelites' fortunes changed. Seti I (1309—1290 B.C.) began a great building program in the delta of the Nile. The Israelites were living close by in Goshen. By this time, the memory of Joseph, the Israelite, who had saved Egypt in time of famine when the Hyksos were in control, had become rather dim if not almost forgotten. Seti had no interest in the Semitic peoples living in his land, other than to use them to further his building projects. He was interested in making Egypt a great empire.

Exodus and Numbers record that the Israelites were used to build Pharaoh's "treasure cities, Pithom and Rameses" (Exod. 1:11; 12:37; Num. 33:3, 5). Thus it came about that Seti made slaves of the Hebrews and used them for his building projects. In doing so he accomplished two things: He found the necessary human labor he needed, and at the same time made it difficult for these Semitic foreigners in his land to kindle any uprising or revolution.

(2) *The Hard Lot of the Hebrews.* The oppression of Seti made the lot of the Hebrews very difficult. But the Egyptians were unable to crush the spirit of the Hebrews. Their manner of living seemed to inspire a certain awe among the Egyptians. The more they were oppressed the more they multiplied. Finally, extreme measures were taken by the Pharaoh. He ordered the destruction of all male babies. This act on the part of the Egyptian ruler was in effect an act against God. From this point on it is a contest between the will and purposes of the Pharaoh and the will and purposes of God for his people.

2. *The Title.* The book derives its name from the "going out" or exodus of the Israelites from Egypt. The

Hebrews originally referred to this book by its initial words, as was their custom with all of the books of the Pentateuch, but later the title "Exodus" was given it because of the central event which is its theme.

3. *The Purpose*. The general purpose is to continue the account of how God unfolded his purpose and selected the Hebrews from all the peoples of the world, in order to reveal himself to them, and they in turn to communicate that knowledge to other peoples.

Specifically, the purpose is to give an account of those historic events upon which the faith of Israel is based. There must be no question about that faith resting upon historical revelation. The decisive act of God in bringing liberation to the Hebrews is the dominant theme. But the purpose is further to show how God established them as a community, placed them under the Mosaic covenant, and set up religious institutions and regulations.

But behind all this was the central purpose of the entire Old Testament of choosing a special people to whom God would reveal himself and his purpose for the redemption of the world. The culmination of this purpose is reached in the coming of Jesus Christ.

4. *The Contents of the Book*. Here space will permit us to list only the main events, leaving the reader to fill in the details from the reading of the book, and from the use of other source materials such as those suggested at the end of the chapter.

1. The Birth and Early Life of Moses
2. Moses Identifies Himself with the Hebrews; He Becomes an Exile in Midian
3. The Revelation at the Burning Bush
4. The Contest with Pharaoh; the Plagues
5. The Passover Festival
6. The Crossing of the Red Sea
7. Events at Sinai
8. The Giving of the Ten Commandments
9. The Tabernacle and the Priesthood

10. Institutions and Forms of Worship

5. *The Dating of the Exodus.* Scholars have debated this matter for a long time. A very early date of 1440 B.C. was held for many years, but archaeological studies over a period of years have produced considerable evidence which has led many scholars to favor a late date.

Admittedly the picture of the situation in Egypt following the migration of Joseph is a complex one, and historians differ in assessing the evidence presented by archaeology and the Biblical account. The case for the 1440 B.C. date of the Exodus is outlined by Unger.[14]

Those who accept a later date for the Exodus usually place it around 1290 B.C. This is the position of John Bright, who gives Seti (1309—1290 B.C.) as the Pharaoh of the oppression and Rameses II (1290—1224 B.C.) as the Pharaoh of the Exodus.[15] W. F. Albright holds to the same position that Rameses II is the Pharaoh of the Exodus.[16]

As already indicated in an earlier section, Seti I (1309—1290 B.C.) the Pharaoh of the oppression, made the Hebrews slaves and used them in the extensive building program. Seti's son, who took the title of Rameses II, continued the work his father had begun on the reconstruction of the capital at Avaris, and named it the "House of Rameses."

The crisis referred to in the Book of Exodus evidently arose shortly after Rameses II ascended the throne in 1290 B.C.

6. *The Experience of Moses at the Burning Bush.* This was a tremendously significant experience for Moses. At first Moses was curious about the bush, but when the voice from within the flame spoke, he became tremendously interested in what that voice said. "I am the God of your father, the God of Abraham, the God

[14]Unger, *op. cit.,* pp. 197-200.
[15]Bright, *op. cit.,* pp. 112-113.
[16]W. F. Albright, *The Biblical Period,* p. 8.

of Isaac, and the God of Jacob" (Exod. 3:6). This was
no new God that Moses had discovered; this was the
God of his fathers who had "discovered" him, had
sought him to speak to him. Moses was awed and
humbled by this encounter with God.

When Moses inquired about God's name, he was
given a very cryptic answer, an answer that both con-
cealed and revealed God's true nature. Moses was told
to tell the people of Israel that "I am" had sent him to
lead God's people out of Egypt. In reply to Moses' question concerning God's name, he said, "I am who I am."
The exact meaning of this phrase is difficult to understand. It could be translated in the following ways:

"I am because I am."
"I will be what I will be."
"I cause to be what is."

Many lean toward the last one, since the Hebrews
always thought of God as a God who acted. This is the
only place where the first person form of the divine
name is used. It is the third person forms that are used
elsewhere. Perhaps the reason is that God could speak
of himself as *I cause to be* or *I am*. On the other hand,
when the Hebrew spoke of God he could say *He causes
to be*. The Hebrew name for God is Yahweh, and it is
the third person form.

Moses and the Hebrew people were to discover the
meaning of God, not by pondering on the meaning of
the words God spoke at the burning bush, but by what
God was about to do. The meaning of Yahweh for the
Hebrew people was to be determined by the revelation
God would give of himself to Moses and the Hebrew
people in that crucial hour when he was about to save
his people from Egyptian bondage. The attributes of
Yahweh found expression in those decisive acts recorded in Exodus and later writings of the Old Testament.

OUTLINE OF THE BOOK OF EXODUS

I. God's Revelation of His Power   1: 1—18:27
  1. Growth of Israel after death of Joseph   1: 1- 7
  2. The oppression of Israel   1: 8-22
  3. The birth and call of Moses   2: 1— 7:13
  4. The revelation of God's power   7:14—18:27

II. The Covenant and the Covenant
    Community   19: 1—40:38
  1. The making of the covenant   19: 1—24:18
  2. The Tabernacle and related ordinances   25: 1—31:18
  3. The apostasy and the restoration of the
     covenant   32: 1—34:35
  4. Instruction concerning observance of the
     ordinances   35: 1—40:38

Suggestions For Further Study

Background of the World of the Patriarchs
  Albright, W. F., *From the Stone Age to Christianity* (Johns
    Hopkins Press, 1946).
  Finegan, Jack, *Light from the Ancient Past* (Princeton University, 1959).
  Glueck, Nelson, *Rivers in the Desert: A History of the Negeb*
    (Farrar, Straus and Cudahy, 1959).
  Meek, T. J., *Hebrew Origins* (Harper, 1959).
  Wright, G. Ernest, *Biblical Archaelogy* (Westminster, 1957

The Book of Genesis
  Allis, Oswald T., *God Spake by Moses* (Presbyterian and Reformed, 1951).
  Driver, S. R., *The Book of Genesis* (Methuen, 1904).
  Marks, J. (trans.), G. von Rad's *Genesis* (Westminster, 1961).
  North, C. R. and Rowley, H. H., *The Old Testament and Modern
    Study* (Oxford, 1951).
  Richardson, Alan, *Genesis I-XI* (S.C.M. Press, 1953).
  Young, Edward J., *An Introduction to the Old Testament* (Eerdmans, 1949).

The Book of Exodus
  Meek, T. J. *Hebrew Origins* (Harper, 1950).
  Rad, G. von, *Moses* (Lutterworth, 1960).
  Rowley, H. H., *From Joseph to Joshua* (Oxford, 1958). Somewhat technical in its presentation.
  Rylaarsdam, J. C., "Exodus" in *Interpreter's Bible*, Vol. I.
  Wright, G. Ernest, "Route of the Exodus," *The Interpreter's
    Dictionary of the Bible*, II (Abingdon, 1962).

CHAPTER III

LEVITICUS, NUMBERS, DEUTERONOMY, JOSHUA

(The Early Beginnings of Israel: Part II)

In the Book of Exodus the Israelites were described as "a kingdom of priests and a holy nation" (Exod. 19:6). It was necessary that there exist a community or church in which the historical revelation should be manifested and known. The Hebrew community or church bore a special relationship to God. They were not only his people, but they were to be the community through which redemption was to be mediated to the entire world. It was for this reason that they were called "a kingdom of priests and a holy nation." This theme or emphasis runs through the whole Book of Leviticus, which we are about to study. Here are some of the explicit words: "For I am the Lord your God: consecrate yourselves therefore, and be holy, for I am holy" (Lev. 11:44). "You shall be holy; for I the Lord your God am holy" (19:2; 20:7, 26; 22:31-33).

In the four books we study in this chapter, we shall learn something of the kind of community Israel was, the revelation that came to her, and how finally she entered the land of Canaan promised to her. In that land the Israelites were welded into a nation, and the historical revelation given to them found able interpreters in the prophets and other great leaders. That revelation prepared the way for the coming of Jesus Christ, whose disclosure of God, his will and purpose for mankind, was the fulfillment of the expectations of this holy community of God down through the centuries.

SECTION 1. THE BOOK OF LEVITICUS

Leviticus outlined for the Hebrew community the ritual law, rites and observances, the manner and forms of worship, and the various religious observances which were to govern this covenant community. The Book of Leviticus follows the Exodus account of the setting up of the Tabernacle and the Ark of the Covenant (Exod. 25—40) and explains what the coming of God to dwell in the midst of his people meant for them.

Those regulations and observances were designed to preserve the Hebrew community as a peculiar people, to keep them from being absorbed by the surrounding nations with a consequent loss of the historical revelation and the purpose for which they had been called as a chosen community of God.

1. *The Title.* Our title Leviticus, for the third book of the Pentateuch, is borrowed from the Latin Vulgate translation, where it appears in identical form. The Latin title is based on the title in the Greek translation, *Leueitikon,* meaning Levitical. This title attempts to describe the contents of the book, which is a book of ritual dealing with the worship and service of the Tabernacle and the Hebrew community.

The writers of the Jewish Talmud designated Leviticus as the "Law of the Priests." In the Hebrew Old Testament it is designated by the opening word of the Hebrew text, *Wayyiqra,* "and he called." This has led to the book being spoken of as "The Book of the Called."

2. *The Purpose.* Leviticus is an integral part of the Pentateuch, and as such shares the general purpose of the Pentateuch. That purpose was to show how God chose the Hebrews as his own people, a holy nation and a kingdom of priests, through which the divine revelation was to be made known in all the earth. There was a special covenant relationship between God and his people, and the nature of that relationship, and

the laws and regulations involved in it are defined in the Pentateuch.

The purpose of Leviticus is to set forth and classify the laws which were to regulate principally the religious life of the new nation. It outlines for the Hebrews the way of approach to God.

Those who hold to the late origin of Leviticus as part of the P source, during the exile (587—538 B.C.), explain that the purpose of that code was "to show how the only God in existence became the invisible sovereign of the Jewish community. From the moment God created heaven and earth, this one purpose, according to 'P' was to separate Israel from the other nations, reveal his Law, give his covenant, and provide a country for it."¹ Leviticus then describes the constitution and statutes of this theocratic state.

A more conservative point of view suggests that the purpose described above is inherent in the early, original Mosaic legislation. Even if the Book of Leviticus did not appear in its present form as we have it today until after the Exile, that does not necessarily indicate that the basic ideas and general contents originated at that time. There can be no question but that Leviticus does preserve in a number of instances the ancient wilderness situation associated with the Tabernacle and its services. Basic materials and concepts were likely transmitted orally until they became part of the written record.

3. *Theme and General Contents.* The last verses of Exodus (40:34-38) set the stage for understanding the theme of the book and the nature of its contents. Those verses describe Yahweh's coming to take up his abode in the Tabernacle in the very midst of his people. This was a most significant event. How were the Israelites to conduct themselves in the presence of God? What was

¹Robert H. Pfeiffer, *Introduction to the Old Testament*, p. 191.

to be their relationship with him? The answers are given in four main divisions of the book.

I. Ritual related to Israel's approach to God.   chaps. 1— 7

II. Ordination of the priests who will serve as mediators between man and God.   chaps. 8—10

III. Laws regulating to purification.   chaps. 11—15

IV. The Holiness Code. This describes the moral laws governing the conduct of the Hebrews in whose midst the Holy God dwells. The basic law is stated in 19:18: "Thou shalt love thy neighbor as thyself."   chaps. 17—26

4. *The Religious and Theological Teachings.*

(1) *The Holiness of God and Man.* About one half of the Book of Leviticus lays emphasis on the holiness of God. Holiness was the very essence of His being. Rites, persons, and places were holy because they were related to God, and therefore derived their holiness from him. However, when it came to the holiness of the people, they were considered holy not only because they were the chosen people of God and related to him by the covenant, but also by reason of their obedience to him and to the Law of Holiness, especially that contained in chapters 16—26. They were enjoined, therefore, to be holy as God is holy.

(2) *The Doctrine of Sin.* The conception of sin in the Old Testament has been summarized as "the personal violation of one's relationship with God, as the involvement of one's whole being in a haughty and rebellious act." This concept of sin grows out of the knowledge that man and his life are related to God. Failure to maintain that relationship, or an action or attitude that violated or disrupted that relationship, was sin which brought guilt and judgment.

While the above definition is not clearly stated in the Book of Leviticus, the entire Levitical system, with its offerings and sacrifices, its sin offerings and its observance of the Day of Atonement, served to create in the Hebrew a keen awareness of sin.

(3) *A Doctrine of Atonement.* The sacrificial system was instituted to give assurance to the Hebrew that there was a means of atonement whereby the breach between man and God could be healed. The idea of "covering" is associated with the word "atonement." Man's sin stood between him and God. But the atonement "covered" man's sin and made possible reconciliation with God. But we must not separate the idea of substitution, whereby man can provide another life, the life of an animal, to be offered up in place of his own life. And with the concept of covering and substitution one must include forgiveness and reconciliation, which are also implied in the sacrificial system.

Section 2. The Book of Numbers

Numbers is the fourth book or division of the Pentateuch, and as such logically follows Leviticus. From our study of Genesis and Exodus we came to understand the origins of the Hebrew community and how they came to be chosen by God as his covenant people or nation. Leviticus explained the nature of this people as a holy nation and as a kingdom of priests. It is left to the Book of Numbers to outline the organization of the new community, who their leaders were, how the land was to be divided among them, the source of authority, and how the nation was to be supported.

The book contains both historical and legislative material. The historical narrative portion of the Pentateuch ended with the Book of Exodus with the Hebrews camped at Sinai. Leviticus, therefore, may be considered as a parenthesis, for a pause is made in the narrative to explain and define the laws that were to govern the religious life of the new nation. With the Book of Numbers the Hebrews are ready to resume their journey, and it is at this point that the book resumes the historical narrative.

1. *The Title.* The title "Numbers" comes to us in English from the Latin Vulgate, where the title is *Liber Numeri.* That is a translation from the Greek Septuagint, which has the title *Arithmoi.* This title was given, no doubt, because of the censuses that were taken of the people, the first numbering having been taken when they had ended their stay at Sinai, and the other at the beginning of the encampment on the plains of Moab about thirty-eight years later.

The Hebrews usually designate their fourth division of the Pentateuch by the fifth word of the book, *bemidhbar,* meaning "in the wilderness." Sometimes they follow their usual custom and designate it by the first word *wayedhabber,* meaning "and he [Yahweh] said."

2. *The Purpose.* The primary purpose is to continue the historical narrative of the Hebrews from the point where it was left at the close of the Book of Exodus. The narrative is made up of specially selected events, for there is no suggestion that it is a complete record of what happened during the period of about thirty-nine years.

A second purpose, however, is to show how God continued to reveal himself in special acts to aid his people and to preserve them as his community. The decisive act of the Exodus, which delivered them from enslavement in Egypt, was never forgotten and was the central fact of their history. But God continued to manifest himself in their behalf, and the Book of Numbers reveals something of that redeeming activity of God, whether it be the temporal provision of food, or the guidance provided by the pillar of fire and the cloud, or his judgment and discipline.

3. *Theme and General Contents.* The theme of the book has to do mainly with the social organization of the community and the record of events on their march from Sinai to the plains of Moab. The way the author

outlines the division of duties, the way the people are numbered, the tax system, the allotment of land, and the establishment of a hierarchy of authoritative leaders indicates an interest in making the Israelites realize how important it was for them to be a closely knit community, subject to the leaders God has appointed.

An analysis of the contents can be made according to the places where the principal events took place. On that basis there would be three divisions.

I. Arrangements for leaving Sinai. These events took place within one year from the Exodus and the arrival at Sinai.   chaps. 1— 9

II. Events that took place between their leaving Sinai and the arrival on the plains of Moab, north and east of the Dead Sea on Transjordan.   chaps. 10—21

III. Events that took place on the plains of Moab while preparations were being made for the invasion of Canaan, across the Jordan River.   chaps. 23—36

4. *The Religious and Theological Teachings.*

(1) *The Redemptive Action of Yahweh.* Reference has already been made above to the redemptive activity of God as disclosed in the Book of Numbers. This was a tremendous power and influence in the life of the community, for when dissension arose and the struggle for leadership became intense, when the people murmured and complained because there was no food or water, the thing that held them together was the consciousness that God had acted and was continuing to act in their behalf to redeem and save them.

(2) *The Invisible Presence.* During the thirty-nine years in the vicinity of Kadesh, the tent of meeting or the Tabernacle stood in their midst as a reminder of the presence of Yahweh with them. In the Most Holy Place was the Ark of the Covenant. The Hebrews were deeply convinced that the invisible and holy God made his presence manifest above the Ark. To them "Yah-

weh was worshiped as the transcendent God who dwells in heaven and who also, without any limitation upon his sovereignty, dwells in the midst of his people as their leader."[2]

SECTION 3. THE BOOK OF DEUTERONOMY

Students of Deuteronomy have called it a great sermon or a series of sermons, and have spoken of it as Israel's first homiletical literature. "The book has a notable style," says Irwin. "If one were obliged to characterize it in a single term, that word would be 'flow'; it has a rounded fluency, a rhythmic dignity, that imparts majesty and elevation. The author delights in words, in their cadences and overtones. He piles them up in synonyms, he entwines them in ornate patterns, he balances them in polished phrases, until at times, half entranced with their music, he almost loses his line of thought in their enchanting beauty. . . . Through his balance and rhythm, his sense of form and proportion, and in his love of the allusive, pictorial quality of words, his prose becomes lyric."[3]

The book exercised a tremendous influence upon the life of Israel. It was the basic teachings of this book, found in the Temple in 621, which produced, during the reign of Josiah, the most radical reformation imaginable. "Its effects," says Dr. Bewer, "were not only immediate, but far-reaching. Religion now had an authoritative book around which it centered more and more. It could be taught. Men were exhorted to study it day and night, to think of it at home and abroad, to teach it to their children."[4]

1. *The Title.* The book was named by the Greek translators of the Septuagint, *deuteros nomos,* or sec-

[2]Anderson, *op. cit.,* pp. 65-66.

[3]William A. Irwin, "The Literature of the Old Testament" in *The Interpreter's Bible,* I., p. 182.

[4]*Introduction to the Literature of the Old Testament,* pp. 134-135.

ond law. It is from the Greek title that we have derived our English name, Deuteronomy. Because the book recapitulates the history of Israel, along with a partial repetition and explanation of the laws given, it has been explained as a repetition or copy of the law. But it is more than a mere repetition. It is a commentary or explanation of Israel's laws and her history from the standpoint of the law of love. See Deuteronomy 6:5.

The Jews sometimes referred to this fifth division of the Pentateuch as the "repetition of the Law," but, following the usual custom, the Hebrew Old Testament titles it with the use of the first words of the book, *Elleh haddevarim,* "these are the words." Sometimes the shorter form *Devarim,* "words," is used.

2. *The Problem of Authorship.* There has been a great deal of discussion with regard to the author of this book. Those who hold to the Mosaic authorship point out that the book itself names Moses as the writer (Deut. 31:9, 24-26, 30; 32). Its background of conquest, its description of a pilgrim people ready to enter the land of Canaan, and the general scope and spirit of the writing suggest the Mosaic age.

On the other hand there are those who feel that although Moses did not write the book as we have it today, the atmosphere of the book is that of the Mosaic faith. They see in the book a revival of Mosaic teaching, and a call to the people of Israel to return to the original faith of the Mosaic period.

A study of Second Kings 22—23, where the reforms under Josiah are described, shows a striking similarity between those reforms and the provisions made in the Book of Deuteronomy. This has led to the conclusion that the Book of Deuteronomy in an earlier form must have been in existence before the revival or reformation under Josiah. Some suggest that chapters 12—26 of the book made up the document that was found in the Temple.

3. *Theme and Purpose.* In addition to what has al-

ready been said which bears on the theme and purpose
of Deuteronomy, the purpose may be said to be to define the inner spirit of the new nation. That spirit is expressed in Deuteronomy 6:5-9:

And you shall love the Lord your God with all your heart, and
with all your soul, and with all your might. And these words
which I command you this day shall be upon your heart; and
you shall teach them diligently to your children, and shall talk
of them when you sit in your house, and when you walk by the
way, and when you lie down, and when you rise. And you shall
bind them as a sign upon your hand, and they shall be as
frontlets between your eyes. And you shall write them on the
doorposts of your house and on your gates.

The purpose of the book was to make the words of
God part and parcel of the life of every man, woman,
and child. It was to make them understand how much
God loved them and how much he wanted them to re-
spond to that love. The following are some of the passages which reveal this dominant theme of the book:
7:7-13; 10:12-15; 11:1, 13, 22; 13:2-4; 30:6, 16,
20.

4. *General Contents.* As already indicated, chapters
12—26 constitute the nucleus of the book, to which
three addresses by Moses have been related. The four
main divisions of the book are as follows:

I. God's loving care for Israel, including a summary of events from Sinai to Moab. This
section is mainly historical.   chaps. 1— 4

II. Moses' exhortation to Israel, in which he
points out that the covenant is the great
proof of God's love for Israel.   chaps. 5—11

III. The exposition of the Law, in which Israel's
theocratic laws are explained.   chaps. 12—26

IV. Moses gives his last impassioned exhortation
to love and obey God. This section includes
the famous Song of Moses (chap. 32), and
the Blessing of Moses (chap. 33). The book
closes with an account of the death of Moses.   chaps. 27—34

5. *The Religious and Theological Teachings.*

(1) *The Unity of God.* There was only one God and he was Yahweh. This was monotheism, and with it was given the interpretation that made him an ethical and a spiritual being. Not only was he to be thought of in terms of the highest ethical character and attributes, but his actions were always in harmony with those attributes and qualities. There was no place for heathen elements in the worship of Yahweh. Everything foreign to this concept of God was to be eliminated.

(2) *The Centrality of the Sanctuary.* Since Yahweh was one, then there must be only one central place where he is to be worshiped, and wherein is the symbol of his presence among his chosen nation. Not only were images and heathen elements to be separated from the religion of Yahweh, the high places where the debasing practices were carried on were to be destroyed. Only in this way could the concept of Yahweh as the only God be kept clear and vivid in their consciousness.

(3) *Social Righteousness.* A study of the contents of Deuteronomy, especially chapters 12 to 26, reveals the very strong emphasis placed upon true social morality, such as family laws and property laws. Thus in Deuteronomy we see brought together not only faith and worship of one God in a centrally designated sanctuary, but also the necessity for such worship and religion to express itself in social righteousness. As you read these chapters note the humanitarianism of the regulations. God was no respecter of persons; the justice of the weak must be defended (15:1-18); every member of the community was to stand in equality before the law (16:18-20). Notice the severe penalties placed upon idolatry (13:1-18), and sexual abuses (22:13-25). The people of Israel were to imitate God in his dealings with them and show brotherly love and kindness. Only with that spirit was it hoped that true unity and solidarity would exist among them as a nation.

SECTION 4. THE BOOK OF JOSHUA

The Book of Joshua continues the history of Israel beyond Deuteronomy, which ended very abruptly with an account of the death of Moses and the appointment of Joshua to be his successor. Israel had been promised an inheritance in the land of Canaan, but Moses died just when they were ready to begin the occupation of Canaan. The Book of Josua, which bears the name of the new leader, unfolds the story of the occupation.

It is not a complete history of that period, but events are selected to show how the land of Canaan was opened up and occupied by the Hebrews. In recording these events the writer points out that the fulfillment of God's promise was not the result of mere human effort or natural means, but again and again that there was the divine aid and intervention.

The divine purpose for Israel, initiated with the historic revelation of God's power in the Exodus, unfolds in Joshua with continued revelations of God's power. This display of divine power in the Joshua accounts constituted "an additional chapter in revelation; God was revealing himself to his people in mighty deeds."

1. *The Title.* All versions of the Old Testament, including the Hebrew, give the name of *Joshua* to this book in one form or another. It takes its name from its central character. The title as it appears in Joshua 1:1 in the Hebrew text is *yehoshu'a,* and means "Yahweh saves" or "Yahweh is salvation."

2. *The Purpose.* Although Joshua continues the history of Israel from the death of Moses to the establishment of Israel in Canaan, its purpose is more didactic than historical. The writer uses the history of the conquest to demonstrate God's faithfulness in fulfilling one aspect of his covenant promises to Israel—that he would give them Canaan for their own land.

3. *Historical and Geographical Background.* The

land of Canaan, whose occupation by the Hebrews
began under Joshua, was part of the area known as the
Fertile Crescent. It is an area just at the edge of the
Arabian desert and stretches from the Persian Gulf on
the east, up through the fertile plains of the Tigris and
Euphrates rivers, curving down through Syria and Palestine toward Egypt and the Nile river. This rich and
fruitful area was the cradle of ancient civilization before the Israelites entered the picture. Canaan lay between Egypt and Mesopotamia and was strategically
important for any power seeking to make conquest of
those areas that made up the Fertile Crescent. From
about the time of Abraham the land of Canaan had
been more or less under the control or influence of
Egypt. The extent of Egypt's control over Canaan depended upon her ability to cope with the powers that
sought to weaken Egypt. At the time, the Hebrews,
under the leadership of Joshua, made their initial entry
into Canaan, the Egyptians were busy with their foes
and could pay no attention to the Hebrews.

This brief summary provides the background for the
sudden conquest of the hill country of Canaan under
Joshua. This initial conquest had to be followed up
after the death of Joshua by a continual battle for the
land. Judges 1:19 points out the difficulty confronting
the Israelites: "And the Lord was with Judah, and he
took possession of the hill country, but he could not
drive out the inhabitants of the plain, because they had
chariots of iron." All evidence points to the fact that
during this period of Joshua the Israelites did take from
the Canaanites a large portion of the central hill country of Canaan.

4. *The Problem of Chronology.* The dating of the
events recorded in the Book of Joshua is tied up with
the dating of Exodus, already discussed in the former
chapter. The date of 1290 B.C. for the Exodus, suggested by Albright, has received wide acceptance. On
that basis the events in Joshua are usually set beginning

with 1250 B.C. Bright gives 1250—1200 B.C. as the period of Israelite conquest of Palestine. Archaeological findings indicate that the Israelites were in Palestine in considerable force before 1230 B.C. Joshua's conquest of Canaan followed two main lines of operation, one in the north and one in the south. In the south were such towns as Jericho, Lachish, Debir, Eglon, and Libnah. Archaeological work has been carried on in nearly all these places, with the result that scholars have concluded there was considerable destruction in them about 1250 B.C.[5] Recent excavations at Hazor in the north (see Josh. 11:10) reveal continuous occupation of that place by the Canaanites until the middle of the thirteenth century before Christ, which fits the pattern of Joshua's conquest.

5. *General Contents*. The material falls into three parts:

I. The conquest of the land.	chaps. 1—12
II. The allocation of territory among the tribes.	chaps. 13—21
III. The return of the Eastern tribes to East Jordan and Joshua's farewell address and death.	chaps. 22—24

Attention is called to chapter 24, where a solemn ceremony is described. This assembly and ceremony was held at Shechem, close to Jacob's grave and Jacob's well. Archaeologists have uncovered the remains of this ancient city, close to the modern city of Nablus. Here Joshua rehearsed Israel's history, beginning with the patriarchs and then emphasizing especially the events associated with the Exodus and with the conquest of Canaan. This was, in fact, a renewal of the Sinai covenant. But it was possibly something more.

It is supposed that there dwelt in the region around Shechem relatives of the Israelites who remained in

---

[5]Thompson, *op. cit.*, chap. 4.

Canaan (see Gen. 34) when their brethren under Jacob went down into Egypt. This may account for the fact that nothing is said in Joshua about the conquest of Shechem. The residents likely welcomed the invading Israelites and associated themselves with them. If this theory is true, then the solemn renewal of the covenant at Shechem was also a means whereby Joshua extended the benefits of the covenant to the new people. John Bright thinks that friendly Canaanites, converted to Yahweh, were also included in this solemn ceremony.[6]

6. *Religious and Theological Teachings.*

(1) *Belief in the Presence of Yahweh.* The Book of Joshua reveals an intense awareness and deep conviction that the achievements in connection with the Israelites' entering the land of Canaan were due to the presence of Yahweh with them. They believed that God actively participated in their struggle and led them into the land promised them. All of this was to enable them, as the chosen community, to fulfill their historic mission in the world. This sense of God's presence and the deep conviction of their mission welded them together and filled them with that zeal so evident in Joshua.

(2) *The Covenant and the Covenant Community.* Attention has already been called to the renewal of the covenant ceremony at Shechem. At that ceremony the people responded by declaring, "We will serve Yahweh, for he is our God." In this ceremony the Israelite community reaffirmed its belief, a belief that had come to them through Moses, that for them there could be only one God.

It is supposed that a recital of the covenant took place whenever a festival was held at Shechem, where the central sanctuary was located. Later the sanctuary was moved to Shiloh. The people recognized that the

[6] *A History of Israel,* p. 122.

laws God had given Israel were part of the covenant and were binding upon them as the chosen people of God. Israel further recognized that the whole of life was to be lived with a sense of accountability to God. This means that each time there was a recital of the covenant law at a festival or ceremony, the people made that covenant their own. Each new generation, therefore, in such a ceremony, made the covenant its very own. In this way the covenant was always contemporaneous.

SUGGESTIONS FOR FURTHER STUDY

The Books of Leviticus and Numbers
    Allis, Oswald T., *God Spake by Moses* (Presbyterian and Reformed, 1951).
    Toombs, Lawrence, *Nation Making* (Abingdon, 1962). This is an introductory guide to the study of Exodus, Numbers, Joshua, Judges.
See books listed under General Introductions to the Old Testament following Chapter I.

The Book of Deuteronomy
    Allis, Oswald T., *God Spake by Moses* (Presbyterian and Reformed, 1951).
    Wright, G. Ernest, "Deuteronomy" in *The Interpreter's Bible*, Vol. II.
    Rad, G. von, *Studies in Deuteronomy* (S.C.M., 1953).

The Book of Joshua
    Bright, John, "Joshua" in *The Interpreter's Bible*, Vol. II.
    Rowley, H. H., *From Joseph to Joshua* (Oxford, 1958).
    Toombs, Lawrence, *Nation Making* (Abingdon, 1962).
    Kenyon, Kathleen, *Digging Up Jericho* (Ernest Benn, 1957).

PART II: THE HISTORICAL LITERATURE

CHAPTER IV

JUDGES, THE BOOKS OF SAMUEL AND KINGS

(Israel Becomes a Nation)

It required a comparatively short time for the Hebrews to overcome the initial opposition after they entered Canaan. The task of making Palestine the land of the Hebrews, however, was a much longer and more difficult task. At the beginning of the period of the Judges (1200 B.C.) the Israelites were twelve separate tribes without any central government, separated geographically, and with petty jealousies driving them farther apart. Two hundred years were to pass before, under David (1000 B.C.) the twelve tribes became an important nation.

The Book of Judges, the two Books of Samuel, and the first eleven chapters of First Kings, give us the story of this development down to the time of Solomon.

SECTION 1. THE BOOK OF JUDGES

1. *General Background.* A survey of the general and historical background of Judges will aid in understanding the book.

(1) *The Twelve-Tribe Confederacy.* Our study of the Book of Joshua closed with the assembly of the twelve tribes to renew the covenant in the presence of Yahweh. Israel was then organized as a twelve-tribe

66

confederacy or *amphictyony*. That word comes from
the Greek term for a confederacy of city-states bound
together by religious ties and by common worship at a
central sanctuary. The member states were expected to
defend each other. Ordinarily the number of tribes or
similar groups bound together in a confederacy was six
or twelve. In Israel the confederation was rather loose
and was made up of the twelve tribes. They were united by a common faith in Yahweh, with the central
sanctuary in which was the Ark of the Covenant, located at Shechem or Shiloh in the time of the Judges.
Later, after the establishment of the monarchy, it was
located in Jerusalem.

a) *The political transformation*. The Book of Judges
gives abundant testimony to the looseness of the Hebrew confederacy. Their political weaknesses soon became manifest. They were separated geographically
and were prone to act independently. Before and during the conquest, the tribes had been led by Moses and
Joshua. During the period of the Judges there was no
longer a central authority. They proclaimed God as
their ruler, whose rule expressed itself through judges
upon whom had been bestowed the divine charisma,
and also through the high priest at the central sanctuary. The unity of the tribes found expression when they
gathered at the central sanctuary for the regular festi-
vals, or in times of emergency when the need for con-
certed action was required. There was some opposition
to this theocratic ideal of God as the ruler, such as
when Abimelech (Judges 9) sought to set up a hereditary monarchy. Later this desire for a king led to the
selection and annointing of Saul as the first king over
Israel.

b) *The social transformation*. Besides the political
transformation, there was also new social development.
It will be recalled that the Israelites who made conquest of the hill country (1250—1200 B.C.) had spent
about forty years in the desert. That meant they were

seminomads and culturally not developed to the level
of the Canaanites. When they settled down to occupy
Palestine, it meant a transformation from the semino-
madic life of the desert to the settled agricultural life of
Canaan. As a result we find in the Book of Judges incidents which revealed the level of civilization at this
time. (See Judges 1:7; 8:16; 9:5; 11:31.)

(2) *Limited Possession of Canaan.* The Israelites
were in control of the hill country, but strategic areas
were held by the Canaanites and other foes who sought
to dislodge the Israelites from their hold on the land.
The accounts in the book itself picture one crisis after
another which Israel had to face. As long as the Canaanites held Megiddo, which controlled the main trade
route from Egypt to Mesopotamia, Israel's economic
life was severely threatened. The victory of Deborah
and Barak at the battle of Megiddo gave the Hebrews
access to this important trade route. Archaeologists
date the victory of Deborah at about 1125 B.C.[1]

Attacks from the Moabites, Ammonites, and Mi-
dianites are also reported in these accounts, and leaders
such as Ehud, Jephthah, and Gideon led the people to
victory. Israel's greatest threat came from the Philistines. They came into Canaan in the years around 1200
B.C. coming from the general Aegean area. They established themselves on the coast, and from there moved
into the interior, defeating the Canaanites and then
making battle with the Israelites. For a while it looked
as if the Philistines would control Palestine.

The stories associated with Samson deal with this
conflict between Israel and the Philistines. That was
only the beginning of the conflict, for the Philistines
were determined to destroy the Israelites. Victory was
to come finally under David, but that story is told in
Second Samuel and will be noted when we come to
study the monarchy under his rule.

[1]Thompson, *op. cit.,* p. 86.

(3) *Canaanite Religion.* In the sphere of religion the Canaanites were a constant threat to the faith of Israel. A great deal is known today about their religion, for the documents found at Ras Shamra picture for us the gods and goddesses, the temples and religious rituals, the hymns and prayers, and myths of the Canaanites. The worship of the Baals and Ashtarts were the core of their religion. Baal, which means "lord" or "owner" was the male deity, and Baalath, meaning "lady" and also referred to as Ashtart, was the female deity. Each locality had its Baal.

In the temples were to be found male and female prostitutes, referred to sometimes as "sacred" men and women. Sexual excesses of many kinds were practiced. It was believed that the fertility of the soil, which brought forth the crops after a winter of lying dormant, was due to the religious rites in which sexual intercourse between the male and female deity was imitated by the "sacred" men and women. The worshipers dramatized this in the temples, believing thereby they were assisting the Baals in the process of making fertile the land.

There was always the temptation to compromise with this religion, and during the period of the Judges, as well as later, the gods of the Canaanites were already finding favor in the eyes of the Hebrews. Basically the religion of the Hebrews and that of the Canaanites were opposed to each other. It was a long battle stretching over many generations. Elijah had to deal with it in his days, but in the end the faith of Israel won out.

2. *The Title.* The book is named after its principal characters—the judges. They were not judges or judicial magistrates in the ordinary meaning of the word, although some of them may have been local magistrates. Primarily they were leaders especially chosen for a given task, and to whom such designations as "charismatic leader," "savior," or "deliverer" could well

be applied. As such they were heroic military deliverers of the people from their enemies. They ruled dictatorially without forming any dynasty, except in the case of Gideon's son.

3. *The Purpose.* The primary purpose of Judges, as with all of the books we have studied thus far. is not to record history but rather to teach religion. As a historical book, however, its purpose is to outline the history of the Hebrew people from the death of Joshua to the time of Samuel. This history, however, is always written in such a way as to interpret the purpose of God. Hebrew faith was convinced that history was under the control of Yahweh, even though he used political and military defeat for the purposes of discipline. Note the principle of interpretation which the writer sets forth in 2:5 to 3:6. What the author of Judges is saying to his contemporaries and to us is that God cannot overlook sin, and that God does punish those who transgress. All of the stories follow a schematic pattern of judgment (or discipline) for sin, followed by repentance, forgiveness, and restoration to God's favor. The several accounts of oppression and deliverance show the following pattern or arrangement:

(a) A statement of the cause of God's displeasure.
(b) Judgment comes upon Israel.
(c) Israel repents.
(d) Israel is forgiven.

4. *Authorship and Date.* There is no indication in the book itself as to who the author is. The Talmud designates Samuel as the author. Since it records Hebrew history down to the time of Samuel, it could not have been written earlier. Samuel was a prophet and a member of the prophetic school, which may account for his being named as the possible author.

On the other hand, present-day scholars of the Old Testament accept the view that while the stories contained within the Book of Judges have come down from early sources, introductions and conclusions have been added which underscore the theological lessons to be drawn from the experiences which the stories recount. In either case the accounts contain an authentic record of the situation in that period of Israel's history.

The Song of Deborah (Judg. 5:1-31) is considered to be one of the oldest pieces of poetry in the Old Testament and composed by one who was closely connected with the event. The song commemorates the victory Deborah and Barak won over Sisera, the general of Jabin, king of Hazor, largest city in northern Canaan and located near Lake Huleh. The battle took place near Megiddo. A thunderstorm turns the plain of Jezreel to mud and slows the chariots of the enemy. The battle of Megiddo is dated about 1125 B.C., and this passage may be considered as having been written about that time.

Students of the literary style of the Book of Judges classify its literary excellence with that of Genesis and the two Books of Samuel. Those three books are said to contain the best prose in the Old Testament.

No satisfactory answer is to be found for the authorship and date of the book, but there is general agreement that the sources go back to the period in which the events happened.

5. *The Problem of Chronology.* The period of the Judges extends from 1200 B.C. to 1020 B.C., the anointing of King Saul.[2] The problem arises from the fact that if one tabulates the number of years assigned to each of the judges or rulers listed in the book, the total comes to four hundred and ten years. This would not fit the statement in First Kings 6:1 which says that from the fourth year of Solomon's reign, when he began to build the Temple, back to the Exodus was four hundred and eighty years. If four hundred and ten years of that period is assigned to the Judges, it leaves only seventy years for the wilderness wanderings, the

[2]Bright, *op. cit.,* (See chart in appendix.)

period of Joshua, Eli, Samuel and Saul, David and the four years of Solomon, a period of about two hundred years.

It is evident, then, that the Judges did not follow each other in chronological succession. They were for the most part local and not national leaders, and it is quite probable that some of them ruled contemporaneously in different parts of Israel.

6. *Contents of the Book.* Attention should be called to some of the important passages of the book.

(a) Canaanites were not yet completely conquered at the time of Joshua's death (1:1).

(b) The level of civilization of that time is indicated by the cutting off of members of the body (see 1:7; 8:16; 9:5).

(c) The pattern followed in developing the stories is illustrated in 2:10-23. The pattern is sin, oppression, repentance, deliverance by a God-anointed leader.

(d) The male and female fertility gods (3:7-11).

(e) The story of Deborah and Barak (chaps. 4 and 5).

(f) The attempt to make Gideon king (8:22).

(g) The story of Samson. Begins in chapter 13.

(h) The Philistines dominate Israel (begins in chap. 14).

(i) Condition of anarchy in Israel described in the words: "In those days there was no king in Israel; every man did what was right in his own eyes" (21:25; see 18:1; 19:1).

The book is divided into three parts as follows:

I. A preliminary survey showing a partial occupation of Canaan. In this section the author ties the Book of Judges to the Book of Joshua.   chaps. 1:1— 3: 6

II. Israel under the Judges. Each of the stories illustrates the theological pattern or objectives.   chaps. 3:7—16:31

III. Events which reflect conditions in Israel.   chaps. 17—21

7. *Theological and Religious Teachings.* The major teachings already have been indicated in the development of other sections of this study. They may be summarized as follows:

(1) *Recognition of Yahweh as Ruler.* An attempt was made to make Gideon king, and his son and his grandson after him to become hereditary rulers. Gideon rejected this, declaring, "[Yahweh] will rule over you" (Judg. 8:22-23). The theocratic ideal was still preserved among them.

(2) *Rule by Charismatic Leadership.* The Judges were deliverers or leaders of the people, who were recognized as such by the people as a result of the divine *charisma* or endowment bestowed upon them by the Spirit of God. For that reason they are often spoken of as charismatic leaders. They were kings in no sense at all, for they could not hand down their office or endowment to anyone. The case of Gideon illustrates what is meant by this charisma or endowment, when it speaks of "the Spirit of . . . [Yahweh] took possession of Gideon" (Judg. 6:34).

(3) *Judgment and Redemption.* Again and again the accounts point out that judgment came upon Israel because of her disobedience, but at the same time imply that the discipline was designed to lead them to repentance and forgiveness, and then on to deliverance. See fuller explanation under The Purpose.

SECTION 2. THE BOOKS OF SAMUEL

Those portions of these two Books of Samuel which come from early sources are considered by students of Hebrew literary style to constitute "the outstanding prose writing and historical masterpieces of the Old Testament." These sections begin with First Samuel 4:1 and include material dealing with Saul and David. The style of Second Samuel 9—20 "is unsurpassed in the whole range of Hebrew prose literature. The author's expert use of syntax. and appropriate idiomatic expressions, his classic Hebrew, ranging from the noblest to the coarsest expressions, his vivid descriptions and characterizations, and his lively dialogue have seldom, if ever been surpassed in the literature of mankind."[3]

In evaluating these writings as history, the same writer quoted above speaks of that very early author of these passages as being more truly the "father of history than was Herodotus who lived half a century later. As far as we know, he created history as an art, as a recital of past events dominated by a great idea. In the same sense, history did not exist at the time, although historical writing, unknown to the ancient Egyptians and Babylonians, had previously originated among the Hittites in the form of annals as well as autobiography. . . . David's biographer was a man of genius. Without any previous models as guide, he *wrote a masterpiece, unsurpassed in historicity, psychological insight, literary style, and dramatic power.*"[4]

1. *General Background*. The outline of the two books at the end of this section will list the principal events during the period covered by the text. A few of the most important ones will be noted here to provide a knowledge of the background for this period.

(1) *Victory of the Philistines at Shiloh.* There was some hope that a unity of the twelve tribes be achieved through the rule of the High Priest Eli and his sons. The lack of unity during the period of the Judges has already been noted in a study of that book. Had this unity under the High Priest been achieved, it would have been known as a hierocracy, or a rule of the priest who would have established a hereditary line of suc-

[3]Robert H. Pfeiffer, *Introduction to the Old Testament* (Harper and Bros., 1941), p. 359.

[4]*Ibid.*, p. 357.

cession for priestly rulers to follow. Eli's sons took the Ark out to battle against the Philistines. The Israelites were defeated, their Ark taken, and according to archaeological discoveries, the city of Shiloh was destroyed. For some reason the Philistines did not follow up their victory and thereby achieve full control of Palestine. Yahweh, who is the God of history, ruled otherwise. The destiny of Israel in the plan of God was yet to be achieved.

(2) *Israel Becomes a Monarchy*. Samuel was the last judge in Israel. In this dark hour of defeat at the hands of the Philistines, he led the people back to a renewal of their covenant relationship with God; he aided them in making the transition from the type of organization they had under the Judges to that of the monarchy, with Saul as the first king.

The accounts in Samuel indicate a difference of opinion with regard to the wisdom of having a king. One opinion held that to have a king would be to deny the rule of God, make Israel like other nations, and the concept of Israel as the chosen people of God would be lost.

The other view seemed to hold that Israel still have a king and recognize Yahweh as the sovereign ruler. Israel need not become a secular state. Israel could have her human king, but he would not be like the kings of the nations. He would be the instrument through which God would work out the ultimate destiny of Israel. He must, therefore, be subject to the Mosaic law and to the admonitions and guidance of God's prophets. This view prevailed and Samuel anointed Saul as the first king.

Saul's early promise of providing the leadership for Israel ended in failure. His defeat at the hands of the Philistines left Israel open to complete subjugation. But again Israel is saved as David shows the qualities of leadership needed and becomes the second king.

(3) *Israel Becomes a Great Nation.* Under Saul the twelve tribes were still a confederacy. They had achieved a unity around Saul which eliminated or minimized rebellion and strife, but they were yet to be welded into a nation. This David achieved.

Saul, by his disobedience and failure to subject his own ambitions to God's demands, became the example of the type of human king who fails to live up to God's expectations and demands. In David we see just the opposite type of king. He is the man after God's own heart. He is deeply aware that God alone is Israel's true king and that he himself, like every other citizen of Israel, is subject to God's covenant. He must, therefore, be obedient to the word of God's prophets.

David was both a great military leader and a statesman of a high order. He broke the power of the Philistines, drove them back to the coast, and established the Davidic dynasty that lasted for more than four hundred years. He not only built a nation, but he also took steps to incorporate the faith of Israel into the very foundations of the Hebrew monarchy.

2. *The Title.* Originally the two volumes of Samuel were one homogeneous work. They were very early divided into two parts. In the Hebrew and Protestant Old Testament they were known as First and Second Samuel. In the Latin Vulgate they had the titles of First and Second Kings. (Our First and Second Kings were known as Third and Fourth Kings in the Vulgate.)

The title "Samuel" was given to the books because of the close relationship he bore to the events of First Samuel, and especially to Saul and David.

3. *The Purpose.* The purpose of the books is to record the history of Israel from the last days of the Judges to the establishment of the kingdom under David. It is history, however, that is dominated by great religious convictions. At the time the books were written the eyes of Israel were focused on each new king that followed David. As each one failed to live up

to the standards of David, the people came more and more to look to God to bring about the triumph he had predicted for Israel. Then the prophets, one after another, assured the people that God would raise up a new David—the Messiah. This was the philosophy of history that had taken root in Israel under the influence of the prophets of God. It was that philosophy that inspired the author of the Books of Samuel.

4. *Authorship and Date.* There is no way to determine the authorship of these books. An early Hebrew writing attributed First Samuel to the prophet Samuel but later raised a question concerning his authorship by calling attention to the fact that the book records the death of Samuel. Events in Second Samuel took place after the death of Samuel.

The use of previous sources by the author of these books is suggested by the writer of Chronicles, who speaks of the acts of David having been "written in the Chronicles of Samuel the seer, and in the Chronicles of Nathan the prophet, and in the Chronicles of Gad the seer" (1 Chron. 29:29).

A general dating of the book is suggested by the reference in First Samuel 27:6 that "Ziklag has belonged to the kings of Judah to this day." The reference to Judah as separate from the united kingdom places the book after the division of the kingdom which took place about 922 B.C. How soon after is not known. It is recognized that some of the material comes from early sources, such as the account of Saul's accepting the kingship of Israel as recorded in First Samuel 11, and David's elegy over the death of Saul and Jonathan, dated perhaps about 1000 B.C. When the books in their present form were written is still a matter of debate. Some would date them as late as 400 B.C.

Whatever may be the opinion with regard to the date and the process by which the early sources were brought together in these books, all scholars are agreed that the books give us a record of those times of the highest reliability and in a style that marks the author as a historian of a high quality.

5. *Theological and Religious Teachings*. The following may be thought of as religious emphases, rather than theological concepts.

(1) *The Revival Under Samuel*. This made a lasting impression on the minds of the Hebrews. There was strong denunciation of the nation's sin, a demand that Israel recover a true conception of God, and a renewed emphasis on loyalty to Yahweh.

(2) *Religion in David's Time*. Stress was laid on the following elements of religion:

a) Recognition of Yahweh as Israel's God.

b) Israel was God's people and his chosen nation.

c) The king was God's anointed. David would not harm Saul.

d) Insight into God's mercy for the sinner. Repentance on the part of David brought restoration. This shows a high level of religious understanding and experience.

e) David thought of his own life as a trust from God. This must have profoundly influenced Israel.

f) David took steps to incorporate Israel's faith into the very foundation of the Hebrew monarchy.

g) Set up a temporary shrine for the worship of Yahweh and then made plans for the building of the Temple. A permanent and central place of worship would be a symbol of the stability of the nation.

OUTLINE OF THE BOOKS OF SAMUEL

SECTION 3. THE BOOKS OF KINGS

The two Books of Kings, like the two Books of Samuel were originally written as one continuous work. The contents indicate that they should be considered as a single unit. The division into two books by translators was made at a later date.

The author of the Books of Kings, whose identity is not known, speaks of sources of information which were available to him, such as the "Book of the Acts of Solomon," the "Book of the Chronicles of the Kings of Judah," and the "Book of the Chronicles of the Kings of Israel." Students of the Old Testament have not been able to identify these sources, but it is known that the courts of the kings had "remembrancers" who kept a record of the reign of the king in power. Genealogies were also kept, and both kingly and priestly lines of succession were recorded. It is possible that a number of such fragmentary records and accounts developed and could have provided the sources of information for the Books of Kings.

Whoever the inspired author of these volumes may have been, he wrote sometime after 562 B.C., the last date mentioned in the books. It is supposed that the writer was in exile in Babylon when he wrote these records, perhaps around 560 B.C.

1. *General Background.* Perhaps the best way to get an overall picture of the period covered by these books is to look at the following chronology of the principal events!

961 - 922 B.C.	The golden age of Solomon's rule. Division of the kingdom takes place at his death
922 - 901 B.C.	Jeroboam I, the first king of the northern division. He establishes idol worship at Dan and Bethel to prevent the people of the Northern Kingdom from going south to worship in the sanctuary at Jerusalem. (See 1 King 11—15.)
876 - 869 B.C.	Omri, king of the northern division. Sets up the Omri dynasty and founds Samaria, the new capital of the Northern Kingdom.
850 B.C.	Elijah's conflict with Jezebel, wife of Ahab, king of northern division 869-850 B.C.
786 - 746 B.C.	Jeroboam II, ruler in Northern Kingdom. This was a time of great material prosperity. Moral corruption and decay developed rapidly, pointing to the downfall of Israel.
750 B.C.	Amos proclaims his message in the Northern Kingdom.
745 B.C.	Hosea lifts his voice in an earnest plea to Israel to repent and turn to Yahweh before destruction comes.
745 - 727 B.C.	Tiglath-Pileser III of Assyria intervenes in the conflicts between Israel and Syria against Judah.
722 (1)	Fall of Samaria and the Northern Kingdom to the Assyrian armies.

In this chapter we shall look at the background of the first eleven chapters of First Kings, which deal with the close of David's reign and the reign of Solomon.

Background material for the rest of the Books of Kings will be given in the chapters that follow.

(1) *Solomon Made King.* Solomon's half brother was first in line to succeed David as king, but in the first two chapters of First Kings we have an account of how Solomon was given the throne and Adonijah was slain.

Thus far in our study, emphasis has been placed upon the charismatic aspect of the leadership of Israel. This was true of the Judges, and Saul also received the bestowal of the charisma or divine endowment. It was also true of David. One notes a change in the record of events when he comes to Solomon, for the process by which he obtained the kingdom ruled out the charismatic bestowal. Israel was still the chosen nation of God, but as more and more she conformed to the pattern of the nations around her, charismatic leadership came to be invested in the prophets, whom we shall study in the next chapter.

(2) *Solomon's Kingdom.* Solomon continued the policies of his father that had brought stability and prosperity to the kingdom. Under him Israel made rapid progress. He encouraged commerce by land and sea, his ships sailed as far as Spain, bringing back gold, silver, ivory and other valuable products. He extended the borders of Israel until they stretched from the Euphrates border to the Egyptian frontier. His empire, his court, his military forces, his commerce rivaled some of the greatest kingdoms of that time. From a simple band of wandering tribes the Hebrews had advanced to become a great nation dominating the eastern Mediterranean Sea.

(3) *The Temple.* Solomon's greatest accomplishment was the building of the Temple. Actually it was part of a building program covering a period of twenty years. The Temple itself took seven years to build, and was the first permanent edifice dedicated to the one true God in his universe.

The Temple and its worship served to keep up the enthusiasm of the people for the service of Yahweh throughout the whole land. In this way idolatry was restrained more strongly than by any other influence, except the preaching of the prophets. The Temple also served to unify the people around a central place of worship.

2. *The Purpose.* The purpose of the Books of Kings is to continue the history of Israel from the point at which it ended in the second Book of Samuel, down to the history of Judah in the thirty-seventh year of the exile of Jehoiachin, which is about 562 (1) B.C.

But the writer's purpose is not to write history only. As was the case with the other historical books, the Books of Kings reveal the philosophy of the faith of Israel. Writing from Babylon for the Exiles he points out that their punishment was a just one. The majority of the kings of both north and south had not been true to Israel's faith in one God. It has been Israel who was unfaithful and not God.

3. *Theological and Religious Teachings.* Since reference has been made already to a number of the theological and religious emphases, a summary of them will be given here.

(1) *A Philosophy of History.* Israel is God's chosen nation and through them he will work out his purpose for the world. The author seeks to point out the root causes of the fall of the kingdom. He concludes that those root causes are religious.

(2) *The Unity of God.* The ethical monotheism commonly attributed to the Deuteronomic writers emerges in these books. Yahweh is the one and only God; he is a holy God and expects his people to conform to his standards. That God is Israel's God.

(3) *The Idea of Divine Retribution.* God is faithful to Israel. The only way that Judah can be preserved is to be faithful to the terms of the covenant.

(4) *The Centrality of the Temple.* The doctrine of

ethical monotheism was to be supported by the emphasis on a central place of worship. This would give
strength to the efforts to remove the high places of
pagan worship and the elements of pagan religion.

OUTLINE OF THE BOOKS OF KINGS

SUGGESTIONS FOR FURTHER STUDY

The Book of Judges
   Burney, F. C., *The Book of Judges* (Rivingtons, 1930).
   Myers and Elliott, "The Book of Judges" in *Interpreter's Bible*, Vol. II.
   Rust, Eric., C., *Judges, Ruth and Samuel* (John Knox, 1961).

The Books of Samuel and Kings
   Caird, George B. "I and II Samuel" in *Interpreter's Bible*, Vol. II.
   Montgomery, James A., *A Critical and Exegetical Commentary on the Book of Kings* (Scribners, 1951).
   Rust, Eric C., *Judges, Ruth and Samuel* (John Knox, 1961).
   Snaith, Norman, "I and II Kings" in *Interpreter's Bible*, Vol. III.

PART III: THE PROPHETIC LITERATURE

CHAPTER V

THE RISE OF PROPHECY

The Books of Amos and Hosea

About seven hundred and fifty years before the coming of Christ, and for a period of more than four hundred years, there appeared in Israel a succession of men called prophets—men who created the greatest movement in the religious history of mankind. The prophetic movement was "a religious phenomenon unique and without parallel. Here we have to deal with one of the most profound movements of the human spirit and with the most significant aspect of Old Testament revelation. Prophets there have been in other religions and in other times, but nowhere do we find a comparable succession of mighty creative personalities who linked the prophetic impulse to spiritual religion and made the religion of Israel a permanent force in the world and a real preparation for the Christian Gospel."[1]

SECTION 1. PROPHECY IN THE OLD TESTAMENT

1. *The Meaning of Prophecy.* A great deal of misunderstanding exists regarding the meaning of "proph-

[1]John Paterson, *The Goodly Fellowship of the Prophets* (Scribners, 1950), p. 1.

et" and "prophecy" in the Old Testament. The popular concept of a prophet is one who is a foreteller of events, thereby placing the prophet in a category with the weather prophet or the news forecaster. Such an idea of the function of the prophet in the Old Testament distorts the meaning and fails to do justice to those men in their position as spiritual leaders and spokesmen for God.

The English word "prophet" is derived from the Greek word *prophetes,* which means one who speaks for another. To the Greeks this meant one who spoke for the gods. The Hebrew word *nabi,* translated prophet, means a person who communicates, or pours forth, the divine will. Thus in the Old Testament the prophet is one who speaks for God and communicates the divine will. The prophet was a person through whom God spoke to his people. He interpreted the mind and will of God. In so doing he might deal with the past, the present, or the future, but primarily his work was to declare the will of God. In interpreting that will the prophets often made predictions concerning the future, but those predictions were usually related to the present situation of the people of God. The work of the prophet, then, was to make known the will of God for the people of his day, though that message might include predictions of events to follow.

A study of the prophets reveals the fact that they had a great deal to say in connection with political events of their day. When a crisis faced the Hebrew nation, the prophet, under the inspiration of the Spirit of God interpreted the meaning of that crisis or the events in which Israel was involved, and pointed out quite specifically what they were to do. The prophets were men who believed that Yahweh was the God of history, that he acted in history, and, therefore, when events in their history created a crisis, God would speak and act. It is for this reason that the messages of the prophets have a great deal to do with the political events of their day.

2. *The History of Prophecy.* In tracing the historical development of prophecy in Israel, we go back to Moses and the birth of the Hebrew nation. Moses was designated a prophet in Hosea 12:13. By mighty acts God delivered his people from Egypt, and Moses interpreted for the people the meaning and significance of that great historical event by which the Hebrews were set apart as the covenant people of God. He thus fulfilled the function of a prophet.

The charismatic leaders of the period of the Judges were essentially prophets. Deborah is called a prophetess, and both Gideon and Samuel are designated as prophets.

The most outstanding person in this period is Samuel, whom we know best as a prophet rather than as a judge. During his lifetime event after event occurs in which we find him speaking as the spokesman for God. It is in the Book of Samuel that we find the first reference to the bands of the prophets (1 Sam. 10:5-13). Such men banded themselves together in order to keep alive their own religious enthusiasm, and at the same time to arouse and incite to action the people of Israel.

Later we see individual prophets standing out separate from the band for the purpose of proclaiming the message of God in connection with some crisis that had arisen. This is seen especially in the life and activities of Elijah and Elisha. They had been associated with prophetic bands (see 2 Kings 2:3-4; 4:38), but in these instances we find them speaking as individual spokesmen for God as the Spirit of God came upon them. It was inevitable that the prophetic movement should develop in the direction of individual prophets standing forth as spokesmen for God, for the bands or groups would be subject to many pressures which would lead them to forget their high calling.

In the Books of Samuel and Kings we come across

the names of prophets whose influence was felt in the nation although their activities are not described in any detail: Nathan, Ahijah, Micaiah and Shemaiah, in addition to Samuel who was mentioned earlier, and then Elijah and Elisha. There must have been an innumerable company of prophets that led the Hebrew people in understanding the will and purpose of God for them as a nation, but we get glimpses of the life and work of only the most outstanding. The names of most of them have not been preserved for us. But the influence of those unknown prophets can be measured by the influence of those whose life and activities and writings have come down to us. "The real history of Israel," says Dr. Davidson, "is a history in which men of prophetic rank and name stand at the great turning-points of the people's life and direct their movements. The inner progress of the people was guided throughout by the prophets." This was because they were men who spoke the word of God under the influence and power of the Spirit. The prophetic movement was charismatic from the very beginning and continued to be such throughout the history of Israel.

3. *The Literary Prophets.* About a hundred years after Elijah a significant development took place in the prophetic movement. Elijah and the prophets before him had used the spoken word as the medium through which they made God's message known to the people, but by the middle of eighth century B.C. (750 B.C.) the messages of the most prominent of the prophets were committed to writing. It is at this point that the great prophetic literature of the Old Testament had its beginning. Amos was the first of these prophets whose messages were written—men now known as the *Literary Prophets* or the *Writing Prophets.*

According to the listing of the books in the Hebrew Old Testament, there were fifteen prophets. They are the three major prophets—Isaiah, Jeremiah, and Ezekiel, and the twelve minor prophets. Lamentations and

Daniel, books which are often listed with the prophets, are listed by the Hebrews with that group of books known as "The Writings" which will be studied later.

4. *Chronological Order of the Prophets.* The order of treatment of the prophets in the following chapters is chronological rather than in the order in which they appear in the English Bible. This breaks up the sequence of the minor prophets as they are listed in both the English and the Hebrew canons, for Amos is given priority as the first of these great writing prophets. The chronological order is chosen because it makes possible consideration of each group of prophets in relation to the particular world power dominant in Israel's world.

During the period when these literary prophets were at work, the four great powers which dominated Israel's world in succession were Assyria, with Nineveh as the capital; Chaldea (or Babylon) with the city of Babylon as the capital; Persia; and Greece. The following table will outline the chronological order of the prophets and the world power dominant at the time of the writing of each.

THE ASSYRIAN PERIOD
912 B.C. (Assyrian Revival) to 609 B.C.

Amos	760—750 B.C.
Hosea	750—735 B.C.
Isaiah (Part I)	747—701 B.C.
Micah	740—701 B.C.
Zephaniah	627—625 B.C.
Nahum	615—612 B.C.

THE CHALDEAN OR NEO-BABYLONIAN PERIOD
609 B.C. to 539 B.C.

Habakkuk	600 B.C.	
Jeremiah	626—588 B.C.	
Ezekiel	593—570 B.C.	
Obadiah	586—538 B.C.	(Note below that some assign to a later period)
Isaiah (Part II)		

THE PERSIAN PERIOD

539 B.C. to 331 B.C.

Haggai	520—518 B.C.
Zechariah	520—518 B.C.
(Chaps. 1—8)	
Malachi	470—460 B.C.
(Some insert Obadiah here, 460 B.C.)	
Joel	400—350 B.C.

THE GREEK PERIOD

Beginning with about 331 B.C.

Zechariah	300 B.C.
(Chaps. 9—14)	
Jonah	300 B.C. (Some place this as early as 782—743 B.C.)

SECTION 2. THE HISTORICAL BACKGROUND OF THE PERIOD

1. *The Disruption of the Kingdom.* When Solomon died (922 B.C.) he left his son Rehoboam a luxurious palace in Jerusalem and a kingdom that was seething with angry discontent. Solomon's fine buildings had been made possible through forced labor and crushing taxes, and the people wanted no more of this tyranny. When Rehoboam was faced with the demand for relief from this crushing burden of taxes, he said, "Whereas my father laid upon you a heavy yoke, I will add to your yoke. My father chastised you with whips, but I will chastise you with scorpions" (1 Kings 12:11).

The result was a revolt and a divided kingdom. Rehoboam's own tribe of Judah remained loyal to him, and that part of the tribe of Benjamin nearest to Jerusalem. The northern tribes, led by Jeroboam, organized a kingdom of their own.

But the revolt and establishment of the separate kingdom did not permanently settle the problem of oppression. After the death of Jeroboam, the ruler of the Northern Kingdom, a strong military leader named Omri succeeded in seizing the throne of the Northern

Kingdom, and built himself a fine new capital, the city of Samaria, with a luxurious palace like that of Solomon in Jerusalem. Ahab, the son of Omri, became king at his father's death. As king of Israel, Ahab took as his royal bride the beautiful young princess Jezebel of the kingdom of Tyre. This meant that an alliance was to be formed between these two kingdoms. It also meant that the merchants of Samaria would continue to grow rich selling grain and oil and wine from the farms of Israel, to be carried overseas in the ships of Tyre.

2. *A Religious Crisis.* When the Northern Kingdom broke away, the king, Jeroboam, knew that he could keep the loyalty of his people only by separating them from the worship at Jerusalem, where the beautiful Temple was located. He established places of worship at Dan in the north of his kingdom and at Bethel near the southern border. There he set the golden calves to represent Yahweh. This kept large numbers away from the central place of worship at Jerusalem, and started the Northern Kingdom on its downward road from God to idolatry.

But the religious crisis became acute when Ahab married Jezebel. Ahab built for her in the city of Samaria a temple with an altar to Baal-Melkart. She then proceeded to import from Phoenicia a great number of Baal prophets and supported them out of the public treasury (1 Kings 18:19). Jezebel was the daughter of a former priest, who was then sitting on the throne of Tyre. As such she displayed a fanatical zeal for the Phoenician religion, and regarded herself almost as a missionary of the faith of Baal. Jezebel came into conflict with the prophets of God, who were equally zealous for their nation and the religion of Yahweh. Jezebel then initiated a campaign to get rid of the prophets of Yahweh by killing them and tearing down the altars erected to Yahweh. Those that escaped the sword had to flee into seclusion. It was a menacing situation that threatened to crush out the worship of God, and one

that stirred the soul of one of God's great prophets—
Elijah. This crisis brought him from his home on the
east side of the Jordan River to arouse the people of
Samaria and of the whole Northern Kingdom against
this foreign religion.

3. *The Prophet Elijah.* The dramatic story of the
contest between Elijah and the prophets of Baal is told
in 1 Kings, chapters 17 to 20. The object of the contest
was to determine who was Lord. The God who answered by fire was to be God. Fire is frequently used in
the Old Testament as a symbol to indicate the presence
of God. The burning bush is an example. What these
accounts bring to us is the fact of God's active presence
in that situation, symbolized by the fire. It was a crisis
in the history of Israel, and into that crisis God came
and acted. "This marks Elijah as the first commanding
voice of prophecy since the days of Samuel and as one
of the greatest reformers of all time. How narrowly
Israel's religion escaped extinction during these terrible
years, it would, of course, be rash to assert, but although we have scant record of his spoken words, Elijah made it possible for his successors, the writing
prophets, in the ensuing years of Israel's decline, to
proclaim God's truth and the demands of righteousness
in accents that have never been surpassed."[2]

Attention should be called to the experience of Elijah in running away from the wrath of Jezebel who still
sought to crush out the worship of God. "It is significant that Elijah made a journey to Sinai, where Moses
had received the revelation from Yahweh after the Exodus. In one sense, the whole prophetic movement, of
which Elijah is the great exemplar, was a pilgrimage to
Sinai, to the source of Israel's faith. The prophets did
not claim to be innovators—men who came forth with
bright new ideas that would enable Israel to keep up to

[2]W. N. Nevius, *The Old Testament, Its Story and Religious
Message* (Westminster, 1935), pp. 121-122.

date in the onward march of culture. Rather they demanded that Israel return to the wholehearted covenant allegiance demanded by the 'jealousy' of Yahweh. They were reformers who took their stand on the ancient ground of Sinai."[3]

4. *Elisha and Micaiah.* The accounts of the activities of these two prophets, contemporaries of Elijah, should be read in connection with the developments of this period. (See 1 Kings 22 for the account of Micaiah, and 2 Kings, chapters 2 to 9 and 13:14-21 for the stories of Elisha.)

Micaiah predicted the defeat of Ahab's forces by Syria and of the death of the king himself. Eight years after the death of Ahab, in 842 B.C., a bloody revolution brought to an end the house or dynasty of Omri, and opened a new chapter in the history of Israel.

5. *The Fall of the Northern Kingdom.* The Northern Kingdom reached the heights of prosperity under the reign of Jeroboam II (786-746 B.C.). He extended the borders of his kingdom to the north and to the south so that the area and extent of his rule was the largest enjoyed by any ruler of northern Israel.

The time of prosperity under Jeroboam II is the background of both the Book of Amos and the Book of Hosea. These books picture the material prosperity of the time. Sumaria, the capital, had become a great center of wealth, and the ruling society is described as having luxurious summer and winter houses, beautiful ivories, and other luxuries that accompany such prosperity. But such prosperity was achieved at the expense of the poor who were ground down in poverty. This also is denounced by Amos in sentences like these: "They sell the righteous for silver, and the needy for a pair of shoes" (Amos 2:6). The message of the Book of Amos will be considered at the end of this chapter, along with the message of Hosea.

It was not long after the death of Jeroboam II, about 746 B.C. that events began to happen which led to the final collapse of the Northern Kingdom. An awakened Assyria began its onward march to incorporate within its empire as provinces mighty Babylon and the smaller nations of the Mediterranean world. Within the Northern Kingdom there was unrest which manifested itself in conspiracy and intrigue, followed by murder and assassination of the kings of Israel, which had by then become a subject province of Assyria, and required to pay tribute to her conqueror. In 724 B.C. she decided to revolt, refusing to pay tribute. The Assyrian armies came into the Northern Kingdom, besieged Samaria, which fell in 721 B.C. and the Northern Kingdom was no more. The prophecy of Amos had been fulfilled: "Fallen is the virgin of Israel."

The message of Hosea covers part of this period, in fact covers the last part of the reign of Jeroboam II and those years of unrest and anarchy that followed. He did not live to see Samaria and the Northern Kingdom fall to Assyria.

SECTION 3. THE BOOK OF AMOS

The prophet Amos delivered his message to the Northern Kingdom, Israel, during the reign of Jeroboam II (786-746 B.C.). The date usually assigned for the Book of Amos is 750 B.C. The general background of this period has already been described. We shall now consider the prophet and his message.

1. *The Man Amos*. Amos is described as a shepherd and a dresser of sycamore trees. These descriptions suggest a man of the working class, more than likely a hired servant assigned to the above tasks.

Twelve miles south of Jerusalem one may find today the ruins of Tekoa, the home of Amos. On the north, south, and west of Tekoa were a range of limestone hills. Eastward the land slopes to the level of the Dead

Sea, about twenty miles away. This was the wilderness or desert of Tekoa. Here Amos and his fellow Hebrews were removed from the contaminating influences of the culture and civilization of Philistia and Canaan. This was one place where the faith was preserved. Another prophet like Amos, Elijah, had come from such a desert place, and with a message as similar and as disturbing.

2. *Background of Life and Thought.* The desert environment had a great influence on the philosophy and outlook of Amos. The metaphors used in his book reflect the wilderness life with the background of mountains and deserts, such as the roar of the lion, the eagle in the air, the twittering bird, and the serpent on the rock.

Amos was from a nomad or seminomad civilization, but his message was delivered to northern Israel who had already developed an agricultural civilization, with large cities, wealthy and ruling classes, and displaying many of the evils that develop in such a civilization. Among the nomads there was a strong sense of brotherhood, strict regulations to insure sexual morality, a high sense of personal values rather than an emphasis upon property values, and other similar democratic ideas. It was out of this background that Amos goes to Israel, filled with a passion for God and righteousness.

3. *Social and Religious Conditions.* The political conditions in the time of Amos have already been sketched in an earlier part of this chapter.

Social Conditions. Conditions had become so bad that there was a great deal of agony and pain. Property values had become dominant, men had become slaves, or the instruments by which others became rich. The rich had become powerful; they reclined on their couches inlaid with ivory, and drank wine from large sacrificial bowls. There was no interest or concern for the welfare of the people, for the poor were sold for a pair of shoes. The rich grew richer by practicing adulteration of foods and the falsification of weights and measures. Their love of gain was so great that they grudged the coming of the Sabbath when they could not carry on their business.

Religious Conditions. Religon had degenerated. Syncretism had led to the mixture of the worship of Yahweh with the worship of Baal. Only small groups maintained true worship. In the south, a large portion of the people were still pastoral, and among them was the simplicity of faith of Israel preserved. Such groups as the Rechabites held that the old faith was the only faith. From Elijah on that had been the theme.

4. *The Message of Amos.* The outstanding emphases in the prophecy of Amos may be summarized as follows:

(1) *The Moral Equality of the Nations.* In the series of prophecies against the nations (1:3—2:16), judgment is pronounced against both the surrounding nations as well as against Judah and northern Israel. Israel could well understand why judgments should be pronounced on Damascus (Syria), Philistia, Phoenicia, Edom, Ammon, and Moab, and perhaps upon Judah. But would she understand why judgment was pronounced upon her? The logic of Amos is clear. God is no respecter of persons. The moral standards by which God judges other nations are the same standards by which God judges Israel. The doom that comes to other nations when judged in the light of those standards leads to the conclusion that Israel also shall face doom. This is the moral principle that flows from the very nature of God. It is applicable to our world today. It is just as true today that God rules with impartial justice.

(2) *The God of Righteousness.* The basic conviction of Amos is that God is absolute righteousness. Religion in Israel had degenerated into mere ritual, and the sacrifices offered were designed to condition God to give the worshiper some favor. The worship of God had

been mixed with pagan elements, and the worshipers were immoral, unclean, and degraded. Personal morality and social ethics had no relation whatsoever to their religion.

Amos denounces such a religion, and declares that a religion without morality is not acceptable. Ritual without righteousness was an abomination in the sight of God. He points out to Israel the righteous character of God by reminding them of His dealings with the nation of Israel, and how He delivered them from the land of Egypt. They could not recall that great act of God without thinking of the revelation God had made to Moses, of the Law and its demands, and of God's demands for righteousness all through the years. The demand upon Israel therefore, is to keep the commandments, get rid of evil, and "let justice roll down like waters, and righteousness like an ever-flowing stream" (5:21-25).

(3) *Monotheism in Amos.* In later prophets we see the concept of monotheism more clearly defined, but that is not to say it is not to be found in Amos. His message is short and he does not take time to theorize about it. But the concept is there in the entire message. God, to Amos, was the God of the nations, and he was interested in and concerned with their welfare and their destinies. To Amos, God was the God of history and it was his purpose that was running through history. It is true that the world of Amos was not very large, but that world nevertheless was controlled by God. And so Amos does not speak of the God of Israel, for to him he was the God of the whole world.

(4) *The Fact of Judgment.* Amos is known as the prophet of doom. His pronouncements of judgment are to be found in chapters 7 to 9. In later prophets we have the picture of "The Day of the Lord" with which these judgments described by Amos correspond. Judgment did fall upon Israel and she was carried away into captivity.

The question is often asked, Is judgment the final word? In the writings of Isaiah and others we see that judgment is not the final end, for there is a remnant through which God's purpose of redemption is carried on. God's judgment always has in mind redemption beyond that judgment. In Amos, however, the prophet's concern is concentrated on God's judgment. To him "the wages of sin is death."

OUTLINE OF THE BOOK OF AMOS

Section 4. The Book of Hosea

Hosea has been called "The Prophet of the Broken Home," "The Prophet of Grace," and "The Prophet of Love." These designations grow out of the content and the emphasis of his message. Hosea is the second of the great writing prophets, and is the only one of that group who was a native of the Northern Kingdom. His message, like that of Amos, was directed to Israel in the north.

1. *General Background.* Since Hosea was a late

contemporary of Amos, the same general conditions described in the study of Amos form the background for Hosea. Jeroboam II died about 746 B.C., and the period of Hosea's activity may be dated somewhere between 750 B.C. and the Fall of Samaria 722—721 B.C.

(1) *Relationship to Amos.* The disturbing message of Amos was still ringing in the ears of the leaders of the Northern Kingdom when the voice of Hosea was heard. Amos was in the last years of his activity when Hosea began. Hosea must have known something about Amos, for in so small a land a report of the Day of Doom proclaimed by Amos must have reached Hosea. Whether they ever met or not, we do not know. One may well assume that Hosea was greatly influenced by Amos, for the dominant emphases of Amos are to be found also in the writing of Hosea—the righteousness of God, the sin of Israel, and the threat of judgment. Hosea seems also to have used many of the same figures of speech and symbols found in Amos.

(2) *A Contrast of Amos and Hosea.* While Hosea may reveal the influence of the preaching of Amos, he goes beyond his stern announcement of doom for Israel, with an appeal for repentance and a promise of restoration. God is not only a God of righteousness, but also a God of love. The following contrasts are drawn between the emphases of Amos and Hosea.

a) The Book of Amos has been likened to the sermon of Jonathan Edwards, "Sinners in the Hands of an Angry God." Hosea adds a much needed message: "Return, O Israel, to the Lord your God" (14:1).

b) Amos speaks to the conscience of Israel; Hosea appeals to the emotions and plaintively pleads for Israel to repent and turn to God.

c) Amos interprets the divine *law;* Hosea unfolds the divine *love.*

d) Amos is deeply impressed by the righteousness of God; Hosea is carried away with the greatness of God's love.

e) Amos was to Hosea what John the Baptist was to Jesus.

These are not conflicting emphases. It is significant that they were both given to Israel in the same period of her tragic situation. Both were needed then, as both are needed today. Both were under that peculiar prophetic inspiration, which is the pressure of God upon the souls of such men called to be his spokesmen. One supplemented the other.

2. *The Man Hosea.* The date of his birth we do not know, but the period of his activity as a prophet has already been indicated as beginning about 750 B.C. The mention of Diblaim has suggested that his home had been east of the Jordan, though it is generally thought he came from the hill country between Bethel and Jerusalem. If he came from the desert area, we have another illustration of how those areas, uninfluenced by the culture and civilization of Canaan, preserved the simple faith of Israel. Prophets from those areas flamed with a passion for Yahweh and his righteousness, and longed to see Israel in right relationship with God. Elijah and Elisha, in addition to Hosea and Amos, came out of such a background.

From the references and allusions in the book, it would seem that Hosea was a farmer. He pictures the familiar scenes of his homeland, paints interesting sketches of human life, and uses the intimate language of the countryside. (See 2:6; 4:16; 6:4; 7:4-8; 8:7; 9:1; 10:11; 12:11; 13:3.)

"A good book is the precious lifeblood of a master spirit," wrote John Milton. Hosea's message grows out of his own tragic experience, in the midst of which he finds the certainty of divine love. W. Robertson Smith says Hosea was a man of "gentle poetic nature," which accounts for the lack of logic in his writing in contrast to the logical arrangement of Amos. "His language and the movement of his thoughts are far removed from the simplicity and self-control which characterize the prophecy of Amos. Indignation and sorrow, tenderness and severity, faith in the sovereignty of Jehovah's love, and a despairing sense of Israel's infidelity are woven together in sequence which has no logical plan. . . . Hosea, above all the other prophets, is a man of deep affections, of a gentle, poetic nature."[4]

(1) *Background of His Thought.* Some have thought that he came from a priestly family, since a number of references are made to the priesthood and conditions associated with it. Though he was a farmer, we must certainly recognize him as a man with some degree of culture and education. Because he came out of the simplicity and poverty of pastoral life does not indicate an inferior culture. In his day knowledge and oratory were not attained by professional education, nor were they dependent upon wealth and social status.

The desert philosophy and the background of simplicity of faith characteristic of Amos, which gave color and meaning to his message, should be considered as equally true of Hosea. You will want to review that background of Amos for this study of Hosea.

(2) *His Call.* Little is said by Hosea with regard to his call. In 1:1-2 we have these words: "The word of the Lord that came to Hosea," and when the Lord first spoke through Hosea, he said to him, "Go, take to yourself a wife. . . ."

Some have thought that the ministry of Amos had such a profound influence upon Hosea that his call may be thought of as coming to him then. Others have suggested that Hosea left his farming and joined one of the schools of the prophets. While we know little about the circumstances surrounding his call, his message is abundant proof that he was indeed a spokesman for God.

3. *The Problem of Chapters 1—3.* The story of the

[4]W. Robertson Smith, *The Prophets of Israel*, p. 157.

faithless wife in chapters 1—3 has given rise to a number of viewpoints. Is the story an allegory? Is it a historical account of Hosea's family life? Just how shall we look at this story? Space does not permit a detailed discussion of this problem. Commentaries will give the various views of interpreters.

The problem arises from what seems to be God's command to marry a woman he knew to be a prostitute, and out of that experience Hosea would learn something of the love of God. The objection made is that it is unthinkable that God would make such a demand upon Hosea.

One prevailing explanation of these chapters, and one which answers the above objection, holds that Gomer was a pure woman when Hosea married her. This, then, illustrates the true relationship existing between Israel and God at the beginning. Why is it, then, that the text speaks of him marrying an impure woman? The answer is that Hosea is writing this account *after* his bitter experience of seeing Gomer prove unfaithful, and after understanding what God's purpose was for him in that experience. In writing his account after the experience, he takes all that had happened to him in the experience and places it back at the very beginning of the story as if it had been originally the purpose of God. This is considered to be in harmony with Hebrew ways of thinking, where everything that comes to pass is judged to be part of the purpose of God. Such an explanation would mean that Hosea actually married a pure woman who afterwards became an unfaithful wife.

4. *The Message of Hosea.* The following is a summary of the salient teachings of Hosea.

(1) *Religion as an Inward, Spiritual Relationship.* As in the Book of Amos, so in Hosea, Israel is pictured as worshiping God with sacrifice and ritual, while the ethical and spiritual aspects were entirely forgotten. In the message of Amos the emphasis is on righteousness,

the effort to get men to conform their lives to the ethical qualities revealed in the character of God. Hosea now points out that the primary element in religion is the spiritual relationship that exists between God and his people. This is done under the figure of the marriage relationship.

The word that Hosea uses to designate this relationship is *Chesed*. It is usually translated *loving-kindness*, and *mercy*, but it has a fuller meaning than either of these words. Love, good faith, loyalty, trust, justice, and righteousness all contribute to its meaning, though the bare meaning of each of those words do not tell the story. They must be thought of as qualities that manifest themselves in the relationship of man to man, or servant to master, between husband and wife, and between God and man. One commentator speaks of this as "a fundamental quality of soul which serves as a spring and motive for all right action in personal relationships."

The marriage bonds between Israel and God, made when the covenant was instituted at Sinai, have been broken. Hosea insists that only this new relationship can repair the broken bonds and make Israel and God one again.

(2) *A God of Love.* Here again the contrast between Amos and Hosea stand out. The God of righteousness in Amos is now defined to be not only righteousness, but a God of long-suffering love. This is the truth that emerges from the story of Hosea's own tragic experience, and when applied to the relationship of Israel to God. It is not too much to say that the fatherhood of God, the sonship of man, and a love that is stronger than the pull of sin is revealed in this Book of Hosea.

(3) *Hosea's Concept of the Knowledge of God.* Because of the emphasis Hosea places upon the knowledge of God, he has been compared with the writer of the Gospel and Epistles of John in the New Testament,

where the great word is "knowledge." What Hosea means by this is an inward understanding of God's character, and the soul's response to that knowledge. So Hosea refers to Israel as the people perishing because of a lack of knowledge, or he declares that Israel "does not know." He means that they did not have the inward, spiritual understanding of God's relationship to them, that he is Creator, Deliverer, Preserver, and Redeemer. Once Israel would come to understand the character of God and his relationship to them, something would happen to their conscience, repentance would follow, and the whole character of Israel would be changed.

(4) *Hosea's Teaching of Repentance and Forgiveness.* Hosea's definition of repentance is "returning to God." (See 3:5, 6:1; 7:10; 14:1.) Forgiveness is illustrated in the return of Gomer and her restoration to the position of wife. In the study of Amos the question was asked whether judgment was the end. Hosea answers that question by showing that the purpose of judgment and discipline is to lead men to repentance, forgiveness, and restoration. Love and mercy finally triumph.

OUTLINE OF THE BOOK OF HOSEA

Suggestions For Further Study

The Prophetic Movement

Harrell, Costen J., *Prophets of Israel* (Abingdon).

Kuhl, Curt, *Prophets of Israel* (John Knox Press, 1961).

Rowley, H. H., *Studies in Old Testament Prophecy* (Edinburgh, 1950).

Rowley, H. H., *The Nature of Prophecy in the Light of Recent Study* (Lutterworth, 1952).

Scott, R. B. Y., *The Relevance of the Prophets* (Macmillan, 1944).

The Prophets As a Whole

Harrell, Costen J., *Prophets of Israel* (Abingdon).

Kuhl, Curt, *Prophets of Israel* (John Knox Press, 1961). A thorough study of all the prophets.

Paterson, John, *The Goodly Fellowship of the Prophets* (Scribners, 1950).

The Book of the Twelve Prophets

Calkins, Raymond, *The Modern Message of the Minor Prophets* (Harper, 1947).

Smith, George Adam, *The Book of the Twelve Prophets*, 2 vols. (Harper, 1928).

The Books of Amos and Hosea

Robinson, H. Wheeler, *Two Hebrew Prophets* (Lutterworth, 1948) Deals with Hosea and Ezekiel.

Snaith, Norman, *Amos, Hosea and Micah* (Epworth).

CHAPTER VI

THE PROPHETS AND THE KINGDOM OF JUDAH (PART I)

Isaiah; Micah; Zephaniah; Nahum

While the Northern Kingdom remained she overshadowed Judah in the south. Israel's position in the north had placed her at the very crossroads of travel and activity between Mesopotamia and Egypt. Up until the time of her fall, Israel had also led in the prophetic movement that ultimately became such a tremendous influence in the religious history of mankind. Elijah, Amos, and Hosea had all been related to the Northern Kingdom in their prophetic ministry. With the fall of Samaria to the Assyrians in 722-721 B.C., the prophetic movement continues in the kingdom of Judah. It is concerning these great prophets of Judah that we shall now begin our study.

SECTION 1. THE BOOK OF ISAIAH (PART I)

We have divided our study of the Book of Isaiah into two parts. This requires a word of explanation. For many years there has been considerable discussion regarding the unity of the book. In our Bible it appears as a single unit of sixty-six chapters, but many have contended that when we come to chapter 40 we find an entirely different attitude and atmosphere. This led to a consideration of the book as having two main divisions or parts. Part I was seen as made up of chapters 1—39, with Isaiah, the son of Amoz as the author. Part II was regarded as composed of chapters 40 to 66, whose author is unknown. The reasons for accepting one or the other of the two positions may be summarized as follows:

For the unity of the book. (1) The New Testament lends its support. A large number of quotations from both parts of Isaiah appear in the New Testament without making any distinction in authorship. They are simply referred to as coming from Isaiah.

(2) There are early references to Isaiah as the author. In the Book of Ecclesiasticus, one of the books of the Apocrypha dated about 180 B.C., the writer quotes from Isaiah 49:17-25, and speaks of the author as Isaiah.

The Isaiah manuscript, found among the Dead Sea Scrolls and dated either in the second or first centuries B.C., is a single unit of sixty-six chapters.

Josephus, the Jewish historian who wrote about A.D. 90 refers to Isaiah as if it were a single unit.

(3) The heading of the prophecy in 1:1 points toward Isaiah as author. It is assumed that this heading was intended to indicate that Isaiah was the author of the entire sixty-six chapters and not of a portion of the book only.

(4) The author of chapters 40-66 was a Palestinian. Here it is pointed out that the author does not reveal any particular knowledge of the land or religion of Babylon, such as might be expected of a person living there. Isaiah, the son of Amoz, is understood to be that Palestinian, living in Palestine when the book was written.

For the division of the book. (1) The two differ dramatically in background. In Part I the background is the Assyrian crisis (about 701 B.C.); that of Part II is the Exile and the period following (about 550 B.C. and after). It is generally agreed that there is a difference in background of the two parts of the book, but those who hold to a single authorship believe that God revealed to Isaiah about 700 B.C. what would take place nearly two hundred years later, outlining the course of events related to the Exile. At the same time God gave him a message of comfort and hope appropriate for that later time.

Those who look upon the book as having two parts believe that one way in which God reveals himself is through historical events. To them the message of chapters 40-66 grows out of the developing situation in Babylon leading to the return of the exiles. Into that situation God steps with a message to the writer of Part II, in which God interprets the meaning of those events for the Hebrews, and inspired the message we have in these chapters.

(2) There is a difference in language and style.

(3) The name of Isaiah does not appear in chapters 40-66.

(4) The religious and theological emphases are different. One develops the idea of God's holiness, while the other emphasizes his infinity. Part I is greatly concerned with the Messianic King, while Part II develops the idea of the "suffering servant."

The question is often asked: "If there were two authors, why were chapters 40-66 added to the Isaiah scroll? One answer is that the author belonged to the disciples of Isaiah, among whom the prophet's teachings were preserved and passed on. When this message came to the author of chapters 40-66, he saw it as the climax of that faith taught by Isaiah, and as a result it came to be attached to the Isaiah scroll.

A second reason grows out of an established custom among the Hebrews in placing their writings on rolls in such lengths as could be manageable when rolled up. The Hebrews used four scrolls for the books of the prophets, Isaiah, Jeremiah, Ezekiel, and the Book of the Twelve, containing the twelve minor prophets. All four scrolls are approximately the same length. Both parts are equally inspired, whether there was one author or two. Since the backgrounds of the two parts are different, Part I is considered in this chapter, with Part II reserved for Chapter VIII.

1. *General Background.* Isaiah has been designated "the most majestic of the prophets," the "Prince of Old Testament Prophets," "Aristocrat," "Christian Statesman," and by other high and noble terms of description. His style has led students to speak of him as the prince of Hebrew orators. "Never did the speech of Canaan pour forth with more brilliant splendor and triumphant beauty than from his lips. He has a strength and power of language, a majesty and sublimity of expression, an inexhaustible richness of fitting and stirring imagery, that overwhelms the reader, nay, fairly bewilders him."[1]

(1) *Historical, and Political Background.* Isaiah was born about 770-760 B.C., and died shortly after 700 B.C. Some have suggested 600 B.C., while tradition says he lost his life under Manesseh, who reigned 686-642 B.C. He received his call to the prophetic ministry the year that King Uzziah died, which was about 742 B.C.

Assyria was the ruler of Western Asia; and with the rise to power of Tiglath-Pilesar III (745-727 B.C.), the greatest advance of Assyria took place. He marched into Palestine and took everything before him. Both Amos and Hosea reflect these events, and Amos warned the Northern Kingdom that the day of doom was coming. The Northern Kingdom fell to the Assyrians 722-721 B.C.

Isaiah's ministry was associated with four kings of Judah. For convenient reference they are listed with the period of their rule.

Uzziah	(Azariah)	783—742 B.C.
Jotham	(as regent)	750—742 B.C.
Jotham	(as king)	742—735 B.C.
Ahaz		735—715 B.C.
Hezekiah		715—687 B.C.

[1]C. H. Cornhill, *The Prophets of Israel,* chapter on Isaiah.

Uzziah was a contemporary of Jeroboam II, king of Israel, and the reign of Uzziah, like that of Jeroboam II, was noted as an era of prosperity for the Southern Kingdom of Judah. In Second Chronicles 26 there is an account of the things accomplished during the reign of Uzziah. The kingdom was expanded, commerce increased, civilization was developed, the agricultural program prospered. Judah experienced a time of prosperity such as they had not known since the days of Solomon. Jotham, the son of Uzziah, who reigned only a short time after his father's death, adopted his father's policies, but Ahaz was a short-sighted king of little ability. Hezekiah, the fourth king of Isaiah's ministry, finally cooperated with Isaiah, accepted his message, and Jerusalem was saved from the Assyrians.

(2) *Social and Religious Situation.* The conditions that existed in the Northern Kingdom at the time of Amos were duplicated in Judah at this time. The vision of Isaiah when he received his call brought to him the realization of the sinfulness of the nation. Social conditions had become intolerable, for the young King Jotham was a tool in the hands of those whose hearts were far from God. Isaiah saw how the leaders were practicing injustice and bringing oppression upon the people. Women had become proud and wicked. The princes and judges had become companions of thieves, grafters, and perverters of justice. Jerusalem that had once been a faithful city had become a harlot, and in place of righteousness murders were to be found. Men had fashioned idols with their hands and set them up as objects of worship. Isaiah pronounces a series of woes upon the nation for her disobedience and wickedness; upon those who accumulate houses and lands; upon the drunkards, the mockers, the thieves, the self-conceited, and the unjust judges (5:8-24). So terrible was the situation that Isaiah said God would come like a great

storm to judge and discipline the nation. It was to be the Day of Yahweh.

2. *The Man and His Ministry.* The name Isaiah comes from *Yesha'jahu,* meaning Yahweh is salvation. Tradition reports he was of royal blood. His message has led to the conclusion that he was an aristocrat and a person of high quality.

Isaiah was likely born in Jerusalem, and perhaps spent most of his life there. A study of his writing reveals that he drew his illustrations from the city of Jerusalem mainly, with reference to the vineyards and orchards which were near the city. He knew well the Temple and its ritual. His descriptions of the houses built of brick and stone, his reference to their entertainment and to the sins of which they are accused, and his condemnation of social evils all speak of the city and of Jerusalem in particular.

(1) *His Call to the Prophetic Ministry.* This took place in the year that Uzziah died (742 B.C.). He was between twenty and thirty years old. The chapter that records Isaiah's experience (chap. 6) is most remarkable, and is only one of its kind in the Old Testament. "It is charged with the sense of God, and nowhere do we find the 'otherness' of God so clearly set forth. Nowhere else do we feel so strongly the presence and pressure of God. Sight and sound combine to emphasize the ineffable, all-embracing holiness."[2]

Isaiah must have been perplexed by the tragedy in the royal house. Uzziah had ruled for fifty years and had come down to a leper's grave. It seems as if God has forsaken the king and his people. The weakness of Jotham, his son, and the threat of Assyria, filled Isaiah's mind with questions. In this mood he went to the Temple at the hour of sacrifice. Many attempts have been made to explain or account for what Isaiah saw. These may be read in the various commentaries.

[2]Paterson, *op. cit.,* p. 63.

Why try to account for it on natural grounds? The man and his message, and the unique influence of his writing, all point to an experience that is above analysis. It makes sense only when we think of it as the divine-human encounter. When we do that, all of the manifestations fit into the reality of the experience, for God had called a man to be a prophet.

"I saw the Lord sitting upon a throne" (6:1). These words suggest a contrast between the throne of Judah and that of the everlasting God. God was sovereign "high and lifted up." He rules the world and there is nothing that can happen that will weaken his sovereignty.

The holiness of God awakened in Isaiah a sense of his own need and unworthiness, as well as an awareness of how futile was the religion of his kinsmen. "I am a man of unclean lips, and I dwell in the midst of a people of unclean lips; for my eyes have seen the King, the Lord [Yahweh] of hosts" (6:5). God gave to Isaiah the sanctifying touch and the call to the prophetic office. The revelation of God had come to Isaiah that day, and the two great truths—the sovereignty and holiness of God—were to be basic in his message and in the religion of Judah.

3. *The Message of Isaiah.* Space does not permit any interpretations of the visions and discourses of Isaiah. The reader is referred to commentaries for such expositions. Here, however, we shall underscore the basic teachings of the prophet as they emerge in those visions and discourses.

(1) *His Doctrine of God.* There stands out in Isaiah's repeated declarations to trust in God and not in alliances or in the instruments of war, his insight and understanding of *the sovereignty or kingship of God.* He saw the hand of God in the affairs of the world, and because there was such a central authority, he urged upon the people faith and trust, which would bring them peace and a sense of security. He is also *the Holy*

One of Israel. Thus the sovereign king of the world is the Holy God.

(2) *The Day of Yahweh*. This was Isaiah's earliest message to the people. As Amos had done before him, he declared that the Day of Yahweh would be a day of judgment against their sin and pride. Chapter 5:1-7, which records the Song of the Vineyard, has for its theme the coming judgment of Yahweh. God will judge sin. Whatever may be his instrument of judgment and discipline, it will surely come. Again and again the prophet speaks of the woes and judgments that shall come upon Judah for her sin.

(3) *The Doctrine of the Remnant*. When Isaiah was unable to secure the cooperation of the king or people, and met with stubborn resistance on the part of a people who had lost their faith, he turned to a spiritually minded group, a minority in Judah. Isaiah speaks of this minority as the remnant. This faithful community of God, remnant as it was, was to find itself separated from the rest of the nation by its allegiance to Yahweh. Their trust was to be in Yahweh, the God of history, who would ultimately fulfill his purpose in history.

It was inevitable that judgment should fall upon Judah, but God would preserve a righteous remnant in the midst of that catastrophe. In them and through them would be preserved the true faith of Israel, and thus they would mediate to the world God's will and his purpose. "God must speak through minorities before he can speak through majorities."

Isaiah gathered around him his disciples and began the cultivation of this spiritual community in the heart of the nation. This was a significant development. Isaiah committed to them his message, whose meaning would unfold or be made plain in the future. Says W. Robertson Smith: "The formation of this little community was a new thing in the history of religion. Till then no one had dreamed of a fellowship of faith disassociated from all national forms, maintained without the exercise of ritual services, bound together by faith in the divine word alone. It was the birth of a new era in the Old Testament religion, for it was the birth of the conception of the *Church,* the first step in the emancipation of spiritual religion from the forms of political life.'"

(4) *His Doctrine of Faith.* Isaiah's teaching concerning faith grows out of his counsel regarding the affairs of state. Of King Ahaz it was said that his "heart and the heart of his people shook as the trees of the forest shake before the wind" (7:2). War seemed imminent. Isaiah counsels Ahaz not to fear, for God is sovereign and has a way of dealing with the enemies of Judah. Trust Yahweh. "If you will not believe, surely you shall not be established" (7:9b). To Hezekiah he gave similar advice. Trust in God alone, do not trust in alliances. Your hope of salvation is in God, "The Egyptians are men, and not God; their horses are flesh, and not spirit" (31:3a), And again he proclaims, "He who believes will not be in haste" (28:16d). Read the entire passage in 28:7-22.

Isaiah points out that faith is the eternal foundation. To him it was the very center of religion; it grew out of the deep conviction Isaiah had of the reality of the spiritual world and of God's control within it. God has a plan and a purpose for the world; that purpose will prevail. The Assyrian may invade, but Jerusalem will be spared, for her deliverance is necessary for the working out of God's purpose. Assyria had once been used by God to chastise the Northern Kingdom and the surrounding nations, but now she was not the instrument of God in seeking the destruction of Jerusalem. Sennacheribs hosts came down like the wolf on the fold, but the miraculous happened. The Assyrian hosts were compelled to withdraw, overtaken by some plague or pestilence.

[3]Smith, *op. cit.,* pp. 274-275.

Isaiah's insistence upon faith in Yahweh was vindi-
cated. This same faith was expressed by a later prophet: "Not by might, nor by power, but by my Spirit, says
the Lord of hosts" (Zech. 4:6). Deliverance had come
to Judah, but not by a political genius, nor by the
might of arms. Yahweh was sovereign.

(5) *Religious Experience.* The supreme religious
experience of Isaiah at the time of his call to the prophetic ministry, reflects his teaching at this point. The
divine-human encounter is the foundation of all true
religious experience with God. In chapter 1 he asks the
people to come and reason with God, even though their
sins were crimson. He assured them of direct access
to God; they could come to terms with him; they could
meet him face to face and deal realistically with their
sins. Out of this contact with God can come forgiveness, cleansing, a sense of fellowship with a holy God.
Religion becomes more than ritual; it touches the very
springs of morality and motivation by inward transformation and cleansing.

(6) *His Messianic Teaching.* Chapters 9 and 11 are
especially outstanding in their Messianic emphasis. The
Messiah is the instrument through whom the rule of
God is to be realized. The hope and promise of
a personal deliverer is always associated with that final
worldwide hope that God shall rule in the hearts and
lives of men. The Messianic teaching is set within the
framework of Israel's immediate need for deliverance
at the time Isaiah delivered his message, and he pictures
for them a brighter day with temporal blessings and
prosperity. But always beyond the immediate situation
is the clear insight of the coming ONE of David's line
who would be called "Wonderful Counselor, Mighty
God, Everlasting Father, Prince of Peace" (Isa. 9:6).

OUTLINE OF ISAIAH, CHAPTERS 1 TO 39

SECTION 2. THE BOOK OF MICAH

Micah has been called "a man of the people," for his book reflects his interest and concern for the farmers who were his neighbors and the ordinary country folk who tilled the soil and labored for their bread. It is natural then that he should be labeled the "Prophet of Democracy." He is best known for his definition of religion, found in 6:8:

> *He has showed you, O man, what is good;*
> *and what does the Lord require of you*
> *but to do justice, and to love kindness,*
> *and to walk humbly with your God?*

1. *General Background.*

(1) *The Historical Situation.* This was the same as that of the time of Isaiah, for Micah was a younger contemporary of that great prophet. His period of activity may be roughly set between 742-687 B.C., for he reports that he prophesied during the reigns of Jotham (742-735 B.C.), Ahaz (735-715 B.C.), and Hezekiah (715-687 B.C.). Ahaz of Judah refused to enter into a coalition with Syria and Israel in the north in order to resist Assyria. War with Syria and Israel seemed imminent, so Ahaz, contrary to the advice of Isaiah, threw himself and his kingdom on Assyria for protection under the terms that Judah paid tribute to Assyria. Samaria and the Northern Kingdom fell to the Assyrians in 721 B.C., and this was followed by military activities on the part of Assyria in order to suppress revolts in countries close to Judah. In 701 B.C. Sennacherib, the new Assyrian ruler, laid siege to Jerusalem. As he and his armies marched into Judea, he captured forty-six of the fortified towns, and carried away 200,000 men and women as prisoners, besides booty of all kinds. Such a military campaign must have filled with apprehension the people of the country from which Micah came. Chapter 1:8-16 describes an expected invasion by the Assyrians. Such is the historical background of this book.

(2) *The Social and Religious Situation.* Social conditions were very much like they were in the time of Amos. The common people were farmers who had nothing but their land and depended upon it for a living. The rich, the nobles, the judges all connived to oppress the poor, and sought to deprive them of their liberty, security, and source of livelihood. Avarice and in-

justice are two words that describe the deeds of those who enslaved the common people. Micah charges the well-to-do with planning through the night how they might get control of the fields and homes of the poor (2:1-2). While the estates of the wealthy increase, the poor are left homeless and without land on which to make a living. Micah suggests in 3:10 that Jerusalem's fine houses, her public buildings, and the refinements of her civilization have been purchased with the blood of the poor.

Religion was as degenerate as in the days of Amos also. Worship was carried on in the high places, shrines dedicated to Baal (Amos 6:9). Hireling priests and false prophets supported the corrupt practices of the rich and mighty, and threw their support on the side of the oppressor. Religion was nothing more than ritual, to which had been added pagan practices. Morality and justice were things apart from religion.

2. *The Man Micah.* The name Micah is evidently an abbreviation of the Hebrew word *mikayahu,* which means "Who is like Yahweh?" His home was Moresheth, a little village twenty miles southwest of Jerusalem in the foothills of the Shephelah. In contrast with Tekoa, the desert area from which Amos came, the Shephelah country was a very fertile area of Judah. It was a rich agricultural country. Here were the fields and vineyards, and the homes of the simple Judean peasants. Micah's city was on the border between Judea and Philistia, and close to the city of Gath. Conflicts between the Judeans and the Philistines were doubtless frequent, and afforded opportunity for the people of Micah's village and the surrounding areas to develop a strong spirit of loyalty and nationalism.

3. *The Call of Micah.* Micah's call is not associated with any spectacular vision, as far as the biblical record is concerned. His book opens with the simple statement, "The word of the Lord that came to Micah" (1:1). That he was as deeply conscious of the divine

pressure upon his spirit as was Amos and Hosea and Isaiah, is indicated by his words, "I am filled with power, with the Spirit of the Lord" (3:8).

4. *The Message of Micah.* The things which Micah denounced in his message, and for which he declared judgment would come, reveal the scope of his message.

(1) *Social Righteousness.* The sins which he condemns are the sins which degrade any society. "Wicked scales" and "a bag of deceitful weights" (6:11). "Rich men are full of violence; . . . their tongue is deceitful in their mouth" (6:12). "The prince and the judge ask for a bribe" (7:3). "They covet fields, and sieze them; and houses, and take them away; they oppress a man and his house, a man and his inheritance" (2:2).

Behind this strong denunciation of Micah is a recognition of the character of God and what he required of his people. Israel had forgotten the covenant and the righteousness Yahweh demanded. Israel had lost sight of those basic ethical and moral qualities in God that are reflected in the Ten Commandments and the legislation of Israel.

(2) *True Religion.* Micah 6:6-8 sets forth the nature of true religion as justice, mercy, and submission to God. It has often been pointed out that the emphases of Amos, Hosea, and Isaiah have been brought together in a most remarkable way in Micah's definition of religion.

Do justly. This is equivalent to righteousness in Amos and holiness in Isaiah.

Love mercy. ("Kindness" in RSV). Equivalent to love and mercy and long-suffering of Hosea.

Walk humbly with thy God. An acknowledgment of the sovereignty of God, an attribute strongly emphasized by Isaiah.

(3) *The Messianic Hope.* This emphasis is to be found in chapters 4 and 6. These portray the coming of the Kingdom and the salvation of God's people. As in

Isaiah, the instrument through which the Kingdom comes is a person, the Divine Redeemer.

OUTLINE OF THE BOOK OF MICAH

SECTION 3. THE BOOK OF ZEPHANIAH

One very significant thing that emerges again and again in a study of the Hebrew prophets is the fact that at the very moment when history becomes most precarious for the Hebrew people, the prophetic voice raises itself to speak of Yahweh as the Lord of history. This fact stands out quite definitely in the Book of Zephaniah. For a considerable period prophecy had been quiescent under the reactionary King Manasseh (687-642 B.C.), but it came to life again through the menace of the Scythian invasion along the Mediterranean coast about 626-625 B.C. The first of this new series of prophets, known sometimes as the Prophets of the Decline and Fall of Judah, was Zephaniah, the prophet of *The Day of Yahweh*.

1. *General Background.* In looking at the historical situation, we find that Zephaniah belongs during the

first half of the reign of Josiah, whose entire reign extended from 640-609 B.C. During the last fifty years of the existence of Judah great events happened in international affairs that had a profound influence upon that little kingdom. The old Assyrian kingdom fell and the great power of Egypt collapsed, and the second or Neo-Babylon empire arose, the power under which Judah met her fate and the people were carried away into captivity.

Assyria was gradually weakened by repeated attacks of her foes. With Assyria weakened, Judah was left free and Josiah was enabled to carry out the reforms so desperately needed. It was during this period that the Scythians, a mixed group of wandering nomads swept down from the steppes of Central Asia, or what is now Russia, through the passes of the Caucasus, and overran Armenia and parts of Asia Minor. In Zephania's day they invaded the eastern shore of the Mediterranean, and their approach must have filled the people of Syria and Palestine with terror. This widespread fear which the Scythian invasion awakened, coupled with the freedom that Josiah and Judah now had, strengthened the hands of the prophetic party in Judah for the reforms that were to follow.

The religious situation in Judah as reflected in the Book of Zephaniah suggests the following: religious syncretism, extortion on the part of public officials, observance of alien superstitions, merchants and indifferent Judeans at ease in the false assumption that Yahweh would not punish them.

Under Manasseh the Temple at Jerusalem had become, at least to all intents and purposes, a pantheon with Yahweh at the head. Allied with him were Chemosh of Moab, Milkom of Ammon, as well as other deities. Manasseh is said to have worshiped the "host of heaven," by which is doubtless meant the act of prostrating oneself upon the roof before the astral gods.

Zephaniah records that this evil was continuing in his day.

2. *The Prophetic Party.* Against this syncretistic religion the prophetic reformers, sometimes referred to as the puritan party, raised their voices. Josiah's reforms did not begin until 621 B.C., eighteen years after he became king, and during those eighteen years the policy of the nation changed little from what it had been under his father, Amon, and his grandfather Manasseh.

However, during those early years of Josiah's reign, before the reforms began, there must have been an intense struggle going on between those of the puritan or prophetic party and those who were mixing the religion of Yahweh with the pagan worship and beliefs.

Zephaniah's ministry, therefore, falls within the period when the prophetic or puritan party was the party of the opposition. If he sometimes seems to be pessimistic, it was because of the tremendous odds against himself and others who sought to restore the worship of Yahweh in its purity. Zephaniah and those associated with him were to have their hands strengthened by the widespread dread which the approach of the Scythians aroused in the hearts of the people of Judah. The work of these men, along with other factors, made possible the work of reformation of later years under Josiah.

3. *The Man Zephaniah.* Our knowledge of Zephaniah's private life must be gleaned from the book that bears his name. There his ancestry is traced back for four generations to his great great-grandfather Hezekiah (1:1). This, presumably, was King Hezekiah, who in the days of Isaiah had carried on a work of significant reformation.

The book implies that Zephaniah lived in Jerusalem (1:4), that he was familiar with the different places in the capital such as the Fish Gate, the Second Quarter, and the Quarter of the Merchants (1:10-11), as well as with the various classes which made up the population. He writes therefore, from intimate knowledge of conditions in Jerusalem and Judea.

4. *The Message of Zephaniah.* There is little that it new in the teachings of Zephaniah. One writer has summed up his teachings as follows:

> The teaching closely resembles that of the earlier prophets: Jehovah is the God of the universe, a God of righteousness and holiness, who expects of his worshipers a life in accord with his will. Israel is his chosen people, but on account of its sins it must suffer severe punishment. Wholesale conversion seems out of the question but a remnant will escape. He adds little to earlier teaching but attempts, with much moral and spiritual fervor, to impress upon his contemporaries the fundamental truths of the religion of Jehovah.[4]

Almost the entire teaching of Zephaniah centers around "The Day of Yahweh." Isaiah, Amos, Nahum, Joel, Malachi, and others refer to "The Day of Yahweh."

OUTLINE OF THE BOOK OF ZEPHANIAH

I. JUDGMENT PRONOUNCED UPON JUDAH   1: 1— 2: 3

II. JUDGMENT UPON SURROUNDING NATIONS   2: 4— 3: 7

III. THE DAY OF THE LORD HOLDS A PROMISE
      OF RESTORATION   3: 8-20

SECTION 4. THE BOOK OF NAHUM

Nahum is the second of the three prophets—Zephaniah and Habakkuk are the other two—who are often referred to as voices out of the shadows. Generally the theme of the Hebrew prophets has to do with the sin of the Hebrews, God's call to repentance, the doom that will surely come upon a rebellious people, with some hope for the future. Nahum is concerned

[4]F. C. Eiselen, E. Lewis, D. G. Downey (ed), *The Abingdon Commentary* (3rd ed., The Abingdon Press, 1930), p. 8106.

with the judgment that shall fall upon Nineveh, the capital of Assyria, the great oppressor of God's people.

1. *The Historical Background.* The city of Nineveh had been a great metropolis of Western Asia for two centuries. She was strategically located in the fertile valley of the Tigris, where roads from East and West met, and over which was carried the commerce of the day. Seven and a half miles of wall surrounded the city, and enclosed what was considered to be the largest fortified area east of Egypt. Her conquests had brought to the city rich treasures of art from many parts of the ancient world. Everywhere Nineveh was known for its size, its wealth, its glory, and its power.

The mention of the city among the peoples of that day brought forth expressions of indignation and hate, for Nineveh stood as a symbol of destruction and oppression. The Assyrian armies had ruined the fields and destroyed the homes of people everywhere with their invasions. They had plundered and murdered. Assyria had become great at the expense of others.

In 612 B.C. Nineveh, the great metropolis of Assyria, fell before the combined military forces of the Medes and the Babylonians.

2. *The Man Nahum.* The book derives its name from the author, who is called the "Elkoshite." His home was probably Elkosh in southern Judea. Nahum, then, was a Judean, and a contemporary of Jeremiah.

(1) *Date of His Ministry.* The only thing we know about Nahum's call to the ministry are the various statements in the book itself, such as "thus says the Lord" and "says the Lord of Hosts." These all authenticate his call to speak as the spokesman for God.

His prophetic ministry as recorded in the book is dated between 615 and 612 B.C. When he wrote, the downfall of Nineveh was still in the future, so his message is to be dated prior to 612 B.C. His prophetic description of the fall of Nineveh is so vivid and realistic that some have dated its writing after the fall had taken place. Bewer and others hold that its message was given before the fall of the city.

Nahum was a prophet comparable to Isaiah. His style is that of Hebrew poetry at its best. "He was a man of consuming patriotism, with a lively imagination and superb rhetorical power. He pictured the attack and conquest of the apparently impregnable city with such brilliance and dramatic power that it still fires the reader's imagination and makes him see it in all its life-likeness."[5]

3. *The Message of Nahum.* The message of Nahum has been criticized by a number of students, principally because of his total emphasis upon the destruction of Nineveh, and his joy over the doom of the city. The answer to this criticism is to be found in what may be thought of as the positive and valuable element in Nahum's message.

(1) *The "Voice of Tortured and Outraged Humanity."* Nahum's message has also been termed "the expression of moral anger." But by whatever terms we may describe it, what he writes and expresses grows out of the very nature of God and religion. He was simply saying that "the wages of sin is death."

Assyria's crime was great. Archaeological discoveries have brought to light some of the legal codes of Assyria and the punishments to be administered to violators. Three included the dismemberment of the body, such as the cutting off of the hands and ears, the gouging out of the eyes, removal of the breasts of women, pouring hot tar upon the victims, and other cruel tortures. That was the Nineveh that aroused the indignation of Nahum.

(2) *The God of Justice.* This is the emphasis of chapter 1. This constitutes a sort of theological introduction to the poem proper. The message is that there is a God of justice who stands within history, and who

[5]Julius A. Bewer, *The Book of the Twelve Prophets*, Vol. II, (Harper and Brothers), p. 21.

will vindicate his truth and punish the cruel and rebellious nations of the world. God is a god of love, but he is a god of justice as well. It is this latter quality upon which Nahum builds his message. We need Hosea's picture to properly balance the concept of God as both love and justice.

OUTLINE OF THE BOOK OF NAHUM

I. PROLOGUE: GOD APPEARS FOR JUDGMENT   1: 1-15
  1. The title   1: 1
  2. God's judgment upon his adversaries   1: 2-11
  3. Deliverance for God's people   1:12-15

II. JUDGMENT UPON ASSYRIA PROPHESIED   2: 1— 3:17
  1. The siege and capture of Nineveh   2: 1-10
  2. The end of Nineveh's army   2:11-13
  3. Fall and humiliation of the city   3: 1- 7

III. EPILOGUE: THE PROPHET'S DIRGE OVER THE
    CITY   3:18-19

SUGGESTIONS FOR FURTHER STUDY

The Book of Isaiah
  Skinner, John, *The Book of the Prophet Isaiah*, I and II (Cambridge University Press, 1915).
  Smith, George Adam, *The Book of Isaiah* (Harper, 1928).
  See also references following Chapter V.

Micah, Zephanian, Nahum
  Marsh, John, *Amos and Micah* (SCM Press, 1959).
  Snaith, Norman, *Amos, Hosea and Micah* (Epworth).
  See references following Chapter V dealing with the twelve Minor Prophets.

CHAPTER VII

THE PROPHETS AND THE KINGDOM OF JUDAH (PART II)

Habakkuk, Jeremiah, and Lamentations

In this chapter we look at the messages of two prophets, Habakkuk and Jeremiah. We shall look at Habakkuk first because his message was given just before the full weight of the Chaldean conquest was felt in Judea, and thus his message stands in the transition period between the Assyrian and the Chaldean periods. Jeremiah began his prophetic ministry before Habakkuk, but since his message takes us down to the Fall of Jerusalem, we shall consider his message last.

SECTION 1. THE GENERAL BACKGROUND

1. *The Historical Background.* Western Asia was once more in commotion, and Judah was facing one of the blackest times in the history of the Hebrew nation when Habakkuk and Jeremiah delivered their messages. The Assyrian empire began to disintegrate with the death of Ashurbanipal about 631 B.C. Babylon freed herself from the yoke of Assyria, and the city of Nineveh fell to the Medes and the Babylonians in 612 B.C. When Nebuchadnezzar was victorious over the Egyptians at the battle of Carchemish in 605 B.C., he and Chaldea became master of all of Western Asia. Judah, which had been a buffer state between Egypt and Babylon, was now left completely at the mercy of the Babylonians or Chaldeans. In less than twenty years Jerusalem fell to the Babylonians. This is the story.

In 609 Josiah was killed at the battle of Megiddo

when he attempted to stop the Egyptian armies from advancing through Palestine to Syria. Judah lost her king and her independence. After a short reign by Jehoahaz (three months), the Egyptians put his elder brother, Jehoiakim on the throne of Judah. When the Babylonians defeated the Egyptians at Carchemish in 605, it meant that Judah came under the control of Babylon instead of Egypt. Jehoiakim accepted this new control and for some years was faithful to his control by the Babylonian kingdom. In 598 B.C. Jehoiakim, influenced by an Egyptian party in Jerusalem, took sides with Egypt. Nebuchadnezzar sent his armies into Judah, but before they reached Jerusalem, Jehoiakim died. His younger brother, Jehoiachin succeeded him. Upon the arrival of the Babylonian troops he surrendered and was carried away into captivity to Babylon, along with many of the best people of the land. Zedekiah, a third son of Josiah was placed on the throne of Judah by the Babylonians, but a final revolt against Babylon broke out in 588 B.C. Jerusalem was besieged and after eighteen months of suffering fell to Babylon in 587 B.C. This was followed by a second deportation of the inhabitants into Babylonian exile.

2. *The Social and Religious Situation.* When Josiah ascended the throne in 640 B.C., the social and religious conditions which characterized the reign of Manasseh still existed. The old high places had been rebuilt for pagan worship, altars erected to the astral deities of Assyria, and degenerate Canaanite cults flourished. On the Mount of Olives was to be found the worship of Ashtoreth, Chemosh, and Molech. Baal and Ashtart were especially popular. Such worship was carried on along with the worship of Yahweh. Pure worship of God was at a very low ebb.

Josiah was only eight years old when he was made king, and it would seem that there was no change in policy in the early years of his reign. Jeremiah describes the situation under some interesting figures of speech. The Lord had chosen Israel for his bride, but she had broken her pledge of faithfulness and played the harlot (2:1-3; 3:20). Israel was like a woman with a husband and many lovers (2:25; 3:1), and the prophet explodes with the cry, "you have a harlot's brow, you refuse to be ashamed" (3:3).

Social conditions were the outgrowth of this perverted religion. They oppressed the poor (Jer. 5:28); murdered the prophets (2:30), and gave vent to unbridled lusts (5:7-8).

3. *The Reformation of 621* B.C. The Temple, which had long been neglected, was undergoing repairs in 621 B.C. when Hilkiah the high priest found a book. He was deeply stirred by the contents and went to Shaphan the scribe and said: "I have found the book of the law in the house of the Lord." The book that was found is generally considered to have been the major portions of the Book of Deuteronomy. (See discussion in Chapter III.) King Josiah was deeply moved when he heard the book read. It contained the moral and spiritual principles for which the prophets had been contending. Josiah set in motion some drastic reforms. It was a reformation in which both prophet and priest were united to cleanse Judah from her pagan cults and establish the religion of Yahweh. Heathen altars were torn down, and emphasis was placed upon the temple in Jerusalem as the one and only place of worship.

This reformation marked the rebirth of the pure worship of Yahweh, for one of its aims was to abolish every remnant of heathenism. With this the prophets were in accord. However, the social and moral reform did not go very deep, for with the death of Josiah there was a reversion to the old ways. The reforms of Josiah were very negative. The failure of the reforms was due to the use of external methods to accomplish spiritual ends. The next few years revealed how lacking in spiritual depth was the reformation. In our study of Jeremiah we shall see how he tackled the problem.

SECTION 2. THE BOOK OF HABAKKUK

When Jehoiakim, the son of Josiah, came to the throne of Judah, he opposed the whole prophetic movement. He murdered one prophet and was the sworn enemy of Jeremiah. The worship of Baal and Asherah prospered, and social injustice triumphed again. The situation in Judah was appalling, and it looked as if Judah was doomed to destruction also. It was a dark time for Judah, and there were dark portents of greater disasters to follow. It was under these circumstances that Habakkuk began his ministry as a prophet.

1. *The Man Habakkuk.* Other than what may be inferred from his book, we know only that this was his name. From the last sentence of the book we may judge that he was a member of the Levitical Temple Choir, for there he requests that the music of his Psalm in chapter 3 should be played on his own stringed instruments. This would also imply that he lived in Judah.

The opening verses of chapters 1 and 3 indicate he was a member of the professional prophet group. These prophets had exercised a great influence upon Israel from the time of Samuel. In the time of Habakkuk they not only expressed themselves as prophets, but they were also responsible for the service of praise in the Temple.

2. *The Message of Habakkuk.* Habakkuk's message is thought to have marked the beginning of a new type of literature in the Old Testament. He is considered to be the first prophet who was not a public preacher. His message, then, could be considered in the nature of a tract for the times. His message is one that speaks to our time also; in fact, the basic messages of the prophets have about them a contemporaneity that speaks to

the situation of our world, as well as one that reveals the purpose of God.

The message reveals that Habakkuk is something of a speculative thinker, for he places himself in the position of one asking questions of God. He wants to know why things were happening as they were to the people of God. Here are his two questions:

(1) Why does God allow to exist among his people such evil and wickedness as is seen on every hand? The principles of the Law of Moses were being cast aside, for "the law is slacked and justice never goes forth" (1:1-4). The Hebrew believed in the sovereignty of God, righteous and all-powerful, whose will and purpose were expressed through events in nature and in history. The problem of how evil and good continue side by side in a world controlled by a righteous God was one that was only beginning to be thought of in Habakkuk's time. If a righteous God controls the world, then how can evil exist in this world? Why, then, does God permit this evil to go unchecked in Israel? The prophet was raising a question about the righteous character of God.

The answer that Habakkuk receives is contained in 1:5-11. Judgment will come upon Israel; divine retribution is certain. The Chaldeans, the new masters of Western Asia, who have come like a whirlwind, whose "horses are swifter than leopards, more fierce than the evening wolves" (vs. 8) will be God's instrument for bringing judgment upon Judah for her evil.

(2) This answer raises a second question in the mind of Habakkuk. Why should God use such an instrument as Chaldea (1:12-17)? God is a holy God. He is "of purer eyes than to behold evil and canst not look on wrong" (vs. 13a). How can God be "silent when the wicked swallows up the man more righteous than he" (vs. 13b)? If God uses Chaldea, a nation more wicked than Judah, to be the instrument of his judgment, then that seemed to Habakkuk that God was

only multiplying wrong. Certainly the sin of Judah was great, and merited retribution, but why should God use wicked Chaldea?

But this question contains more than the use of wicked Chaldea to fulfill the purpose of God. There were righteous men and women in Judah who were faithful to God and the covenant. Yet these righteous ones would suffer also at the hands of the wicked conquerors. Habakkuk suggests that age-old question: Why does a holy and righteous God allow the wicked to go unchecked while the righteous suffer? The answer comes to the prophet in these words:

> For still the vision awaits its time;
>   it hastens to the end—it will not lie.
> If it seems slow, wait for it;
>   it will surely come, it will not delay.
>
> Behold, he whose soul is not upright in him shall fail,
>   but the righteous shall live by his faith.
>   —2:3-4

The immediate meaning of this reply is that the prophet must have patience. In the end the righteous character of God will be revealed, and the wicked will receive his just recompense of reward. That end you cannot see now, Habakkuk, but you must believe that God is righteous, that his purpose for Israel will not be thwarted, and that in the end it is the will of his righteous God that triumphs.

The righteous man must live in the midst of a situation like that confronting Habakkuk, with faith in such a God and in his power to achieve his purpose. The ultimate goal or outcome of history is determined by God. Time is on God's side, for the ages belong to him in which to reveal his justice and to work out his purpose.

Chaldea may prosper for a while, but her ruin is certain, so Habakkuk is told to wait for it. On the other hand, the faith of the righteous endures. It abides when all the vain ambitions of men have disappeared in the course of history.

The Apostle Paul takes up this statement of Habakkuk, "the righteous shall live by his faith," and makes it the central theme of his message to the Romans (see Rom. 1:17). The essential truth is that real life is that which is lived in union with God. That union is one of faith, trust, and belief in the love and righteous character of God.

OUTLINE OF THE BOOK OF HABUKKUK

SECTION 3. THE BOOK OF JEREMIAH

Jeremiah has been unanimously proclaimed the pioneer prophet of personal religion. In him Old Testament prophecy not only reaches its highest point, but also in him the true character of the Old Testament prophet is most clearly revealed. He has been called the loftiest genius who adorned the line of prophets. The traits of character and personality revealed in his story have led to his being judged the prophet most like Jesus, and his teachings being acclaimed the closest to the New Testament ideal. Perhaps the keenest evaluation of Jeremiah and his message is that given by Davidson: "The Book of Jeremiah does not so much teach religious truth as present a religious personality. Prophecy had already taught its truths: its last effort was to reveal itself in life."

Jeremiah's place in the hall of fame of the prophets

is well described by Cornhill: "In Jeremiah we have the purest and highest consummation of the prophecy of the Old Testament. After him One only could come who was greater than he."[1]

1. *The Man Jeremiah*. The year 650 B.C. has been set as the approximate year of the birth of Jeremiah. This is based on the date of his call, given in 1:2-3 as the thirteenth year of the reign of Josiah, which would be about 627-626 B.C. Since at that time Jeremiah pleaded his youth against accepting such responsibility, the year 650 is highly probable.

He belonged to a priestly family at Anathoth, which was just a few miles north of Jerusalem. The influence of such a deeply religious family must have accounted for many of the fine qualities afterwards displayed in his life. Since this family belonged to the Northern Kingdom, he must have been keenly aware of the tragic circumstances that led to the downfall of his people. He was a student of the teachings and writings of Amos, Isaiah, Micah, and Hosea. From references in the Book of Jeremiah, we know that he was greatly influenced by Hosea.

The quality of courage is definitely seen in the life of Jeremiah, but with it he was possessed of a very modest spirit. Bewer puts it this way: "By nature shy and sensitive, gentle and loving, with a beautiful poetic imagination, keen moral insight, and profound religious devotion, he was a unique personality even in his youth."[2]

(1) *The Call of Jeremiah*. The dialogue between Yahweh and Jeremiah at the time of his call is given in 1:4-10. It is a very simple and natural account, but behind the account is the consciousness of a great spiritual experience. Through that experience he came to know himself as chosen to be a spokesman for God. Through that experience he was consecrated by God

[1]Cornhill, *op. cit.*, pp. 98-99.
[2]Bewer, *op. cit.*, p. 143.

for the task, and with it came the deep and abiding consciousness of his prophetic mission.

(2) *A Priestly Prophet.* Reference has been made to Jeremiah as having qualities that place him close to Jesus. The priestly qualities of Jeremiah, along with his prophetic ministry, are significant in this comparison with Jesus. Jeremiah bore the people of Judah upon his heart. Judah's sin and evil were carrying her on to doom and destruction, and the prophetic spirit could utter nothing else but the coming judgment and doom. But within Jeremiah's soul was a deep love and yearning to see his people in happy fellowship with Yahweh. Affectionately he speaks of them as "my people." Thus he identifies himself with their tragic situation, so much so that some have thought of him as a "suffering servant." His sorrow and grief over what had befallen Judah, remind one of Him who with strong crying and tears offered up intercession for the world. In Jeremiah we see both the prophetic and the priestly qualities combined.

2. *The Message of Jeremiah.* Three aspects of the message will be noted here.

(1) *Jeremiah and the Reformation of Josiah.* There is some difference of opinion on the part of students of Jeremiah with regard to his attitude toward the reformation under Josiah, brought about by the discovery of the Book of the Law. Some hold that Jeremiah was opposed to the movement and not identified with it in any way. Others feel that he was related to it in the beginning, but that later, when he discovered the course it was taking and realized that the people were not better off, he disassociated himself with it and gave expression to those positive elements in his message, the proclamation of personal religion.

This latter view would seem to be supported by 11:1—21:1 in which Jeremiah seems to give himself to preaching the principles of the reformation. That activity so aroused the people of Anathoth, his hometown, that they plotted against his life. One principle of the reformation was the prohibition of all sacrifices outside the city of Jerusalem, for the aim was to centralize worship in Jerusalem. This would seriously affect the prestige of Anathoth, for the shrine there would have to be abolished.

Jeremiah later came to understand that the reformation movement could not accomplish the regeneration of his people. No inward change could be affected by legal means. Something more radical was needed, something that would give them a new heart and a new spirit. "Heathen altars might be thrown down but the heathen heart still remained." As we have seen in the beginning of this study, after Josiah passed from the scene there was a reversion to heathenism again.

(2) *The Temple Sermon.* Chapter 7:1-15 is considered to contain the substance of a remarkable address given by Jeremiah in the court of the temple at Jerusalem. The background of this sermon is Jeremiah's evaluation of the reformation under Josiah as just described. He knew that merely prohibiting half-pagan shrines in Judah and enforcing the centralization of worship in Jerusalem had not changed the inner conviction of the people.

The Temple, which had stood as a symbol of the living presence of Yahweh in their midst, and in which Isaiah had entered into his most remarkable experience, had now become a mere fetish. Jeremiah proclaimed that the Temple would be destroyed, and that religion would go on without it. He wrote to those religious leaders left in Jerusalem after the first deportation of the Hebrews had been accomplished and told them they were not better than their brethren in Exile. Those in Exile, he said, were in a better position to understand the nature of true religion, for they would not be able to accept an institution, such as the temple worship, in place of real faith, as the people in Jerusalem were doing. (See 29:5, 7, 12-13.)

Here was inspired insight, but to the people of his day it was rank heresy. Jeremiah became a man of conflict, persecuted, often lonely and heavy with sorrow. But the truth he proclaimed still endures.

(3) *Jeremiah's Definition of Religion.* Jeremiah's great contribution to the meaning of true religion is to be found in 31:29-33. In the previous section we noted that Jeremiah had pointed out in his temple sermon that religion was independent of localities and boundaries. Before Jeremiah appeared in the scene the emphasis centered in three things: (1) Yahweh as the One God, ethical in character; (2) the Temple as the place of centralized worship where Yahweh was to be worshiped; (3) the moral law embodied in the covenant, expressed the character of Yahweh, and the principles of that law were to find expression in a righteous social order in the nation of Israel. These were great ideas. They challenge us today, especially the concept of ethical monotheism. But Jeremiah saw that religion went beyond those emphases. True religion must touch the springs of a man's soul. Only total regeneration could change the motives and will and affections of man. The law must be written on the tables of men's hearts. It is only in the New Testament that we find anything like this definition of religion.

OUTLINE OF THE BOOK OF JEREMIAH

SUGGESTIONS FOR FURTHER STUDY

The Book of Habakkuk
  Calkins, Raymond, *The Modern Message of the Minor Prophets* (Harper, 1947).
  Paterson, John, *The Goodly Fellowship of the Prophets*, Scribners, 1950).

The Book of Jeremiah
  Skinner, John, *Prophecy and Religion* (Cambridge, 1922). A study of Jeremiah.
  Smith, George Adam, *Jeremiah* (Hodder and Stoughton, 1922).
  See also references on the Prophets as a whole following Chapters V and VI.

SECTION 4. THE BOOK OF LAMENTATIONS

The Book of Lamentations is made up of five short elegies or laments. Tradition has ascribed them to Jeremiah. The Septuagint or Greek translation places the following as a sort of preface to the book:

And it came to pass, after Israel was led into captivity and Jerusalem laid waste, that Jeremiah sat weeping and lamented with this lamentation over Jerusalem. . . .

In the Hebrew manuscripts the author remains anonymous. While many are of the opinion that these poems are the work of a sensitive religious poet, a contemporary of Jeremiah, a certain similarity in tone and style with sections in the Book of Jeremiah make it possible to consider Jeremiah as the author. The fact that the Hebrew Old Testament does not list Lamentations with the prophets, but with the Writings, is sometimes used as an argument against Jeremiah's authorship.

The author uses an alphabetic structure, a favorite Hebrew poetic form in which each verse begins with a successive letter of the Hebrew alphabet.

The author wrote shortly after the fall of Jerusalem or upon his return from exile. As he viewed the burned and devastated city, he expresses for himself and all pious Jews the deep sorrow felt over the destruction of Jerusalem. The second and fourth chapters suggest that the author must have been an eyewitness of the terrible tragedy, and the memory of women and children suffering from famine brought agony to him as he penned the lines.

The book contains an important message for the Hebrew people. What has happened to the Hebrew nation was not just an accident of history, but was the result of God's judgment. Yahweh is the God of history, and through it he unfolds his purpose. However, the punishment or discipline was not an end in itself. It was designed to lead the people to repentance. There was a healing quality in the discipline. The judgment was not in vain, for Israel returned to Jerusalem with a clearer understanding of God's purpose.

SUGGESTIONS FOR FURTHER STUDY

Read the book in a translation that shows its poetic form. Smith and Goodspeed's Translation does this and also marks off the five poems.

CHAPTER VIII

THE BOOK OF EZEKIEL; ISAIAH, PART II

Section 1. General Background

With the fall of Jerusalem in 587 B.C., Judah as an independent state came to an end (2 Kings 25:1-21). Nothing but ruins were left in the city. The Temple had been burned, and all but the poorest of the peasants were carried off to Babylon as deportees.

1. *The Situation in Judah.* Only small farming and semipastoral communities remained in Judah. The Babylonians set up a form of government for the Hebrews who remained, approving Gedaliah as governor. Things seemed to prosper for a while, and this perhaps aroused some hope for the Judeans that the homeland would be reestablished. However, Gedaliah was murdered by some of his countrymen, and most of the inhabitants, expecting the Babylonians to seek vengeance, fled to Egypt and took along with them the prophet Jeremiah (2 Kings 25:25-27; Jer. 41:1—43:7).

2. *The Situation in Egypt.* Egypt, therefore, became one of the major centers for the settlement of the Jews who had been driven out of their own land. One settlement developed at Elephantine, now the modern Aswan. Settlements also developed in Alexandria and other Egyptian cities.

3. *The Situation in Babylon.* It was through the colonies established in Babylon, however, that the faith of Israel was preserved. Jeremiah had told them that the hope of the future lay in their surrender to Babylon. He pointed out that Israel would have a future in the Promised Land after the Exile in Babylon.

Even though the Hebrews were a people in captivity in Babylon, they enjoyed a large measure of freedom. They settled down in their new home and began to build a new life. The Babylonians were not cruel rulers as had been the Assyrians, for Babylon had adopted the policy of deporting conquered peoples and settling them in communities far removed from their homeland. This, they hoped, would more easily make them a subject people and kill their nationalistic spirit.

The Hebrews, however, were never wholly absorbed in the general population of Babylon. Family ties were respected. Community life was organized with some sort of religious organization under chosen elders. Some of the first exiles, as the story of Daniel and his friends reveals, were placed in positions of influence and power in the king's court. Many became prosperous and later were able to give large gifts to aid in the rebuilding of the Temple in Jerusalem. It is thought that the Jews were subject to persecution toward the middle of the sixth century B.C. when a king came to the throne who was not of the family of Nebuchadnezzar and who adopted a different policy toward the conquered peoples.

The temptations that confronted the Hebrew people in Babylon were great. The dazzling splendor of the city, the appeal of the refinements of civilization, the attractions of business and commerce, the immensity of everything in Babylon in contrast with what they had had in Jerusalem, and the constant pressure of a materialistic and pagan civilization was such as to make the strongest spiritual leader question whether the Hebrews could stand it. Many compromised and made plans to settle down permanently in Babylon. But the questions which leaders like Ezekiel and others would ask themselves were: Will the paganism of Babylon engulf the exiles of Judah as it did their brothers of Israel in the Northern Kingdom when they were enslaved by Assyria? Will the influence of Moses and the prophets be completely wiped out in Babylon? The work of Ezekiel among the exiles, more than any other, helped in keeping the religion of Yahweh alive and distinctive during this period. We turn now to a study of Ezekiel and his message.

SECTION 2. THE BOOK OF EZEKIEL

Ezekiel was an able and versatile writer. He was a thinker and knew how to write in a clear style. He gives information that is designed to date each event he records. He used a number of devices and methods to make known the truth that had been revealed to him. Visions, symbolic acts, allegories, apocalyptic devices, dirges, and direct prophecies were used to express the truth that was burning in his soul. His best description in prose is that of the valley of dry bones (37:1-14), while the most involved piece of writing is that of the heavenly chariot (chap. 1). Ezekiel has been called the strangest of the prophets. His writing has had a great influence upon the history of the Hebrew people and the development of their religious thought. It should merit careful study in order to understand the significant contribution he has made through his prophetic ministry.

1. *The Man Ezekiel.* Ezekiel, who is called the son of Buzi, was among the first group of exiles taken to Babylon in 597 B.C., the date of the first deportation. The first captives included the king and prominent citizens of Judah. Ezekiel's presence with them suggests that he came from a prominent family, perhaps the family of Zadok, distinguished for its long service in connection with the priestly ministry. It is natural, therefore, that Ezekiel should be referred to as a priest of Jerusalem. This background accounts for his knowledge of and interest in the Temple and its ritual.

Ezekiel's home in Babylon was at Tel-abib on the banks of the grand canal called the river Chebar. He was married, and his reference to his wife as "the desire of his eyes" reflected a happy homelife (24:15-18). He had his own home and there the elders often gathered.

(1) *The Call of Ezekiel.* The call came the fifth year of the captivity (593 B.C.). It was a stormy day, one that Ezekiel could not forget, for he states that it was the fifth day of the fourth month, roughly corresponding to our June or July. Perhaps he had gone to the river for a period of meditation, when the supreme experience came to him, an experience which transformed him from a priest into a prophet. He records that "the heavens were opened, and I saw visions of God" and that "the hand of the Lord was upon him" (1:1, 3).

Out of the storm cloud that flashed lightning in all directions came the voice of God. "Above the firmament . . . there was the likeness of a throne, in appearance like sapphire; and seated above the likeness of a throne was a likeness as it were of a human form. . . . Such was the appearance of the likeness of the glory of the Lord" (1:26-28).

Ezekiel was overwhelmed by what he saw and fell upon his face before the majesty and power of it all. Then came the voice of Yahweh: "Stand upon your feet, and I will speak to you" (2:1). When he spoke he said, "I send you to the people of Israel" (vs. 2).

The similarities between the call of Ezekiel and that of Isaiah are immediately apparent. The sovereignty, the power, and the majesty of each vision had a similar effect upon each of the prophets. The reality of these experiences cannot be doubted. There is something of tremendous spiritual power in such a divine-human encounter that transforms and gives authority to the man and his message. Such was the nature of the call that came to Ezekiel.

(2) *The Ministry of Ezekiel.* His ministry covered a

span of twenty years (593-573 B.C.). His ministry may be divided into two parts as follows:

Part I. His ministry before the fall of Jerusalem (593-587). This includes his call and commission (chaps. 1—3) and various pronouncements of doom against Judah and Jerusalem (chaps. 4—24).

Part II. His ministry after the fall of Jerusalem (587-573). Following the destruction of Jerusalem there is a marked change in Ezekiel's emphasis. Up to this point his messages contained the element of dark foreboding for the people of God. After Jerusalem's fall his prophecies portray the regeneration of the nation, how they may be restored to the favor of God. Chapters 33—39 give messages of promise and hope, and chapter 40—48 give a picture of the new community, the New Jerusalem, with Israel back in her own land and the temple worship reestablished.

Students of Ezekiel and his message underscore three qualities in the prophet: (1) the flaming zeal that he had for Yahweh, described by some as a fanatic zeal, because he was unflinching in his efforts to vindicate God and to uphold his cause; (2) his dogmatism, most obvious in certain fundamental convictions which he expressed with assurance and certainty; (3) his interpretation of God's purposes by the use of apocalyptic forms.

2. *The Message of Ezekiel.* On account of their distinctive religion the Hebrews maintained their identity in a remarkable way. Separated from Jerusalem and the temple worship, they developed a new form of worship which became the foundation for the synagogue. They came together in houses in small groups to be instructed in the Scriptures and to worship informally. The spiritual and religious gains of the Exile may be summarized as follows: (1) *A larger conception of God.* They discovered that God was present with them in Babylon as well as in Jerusalem. He was the God of the whole earth. (2) *A new sense of mis-*

sion. The old concept of being the chosen people of God in the sense of being favorites of his, and which carried along with it special privilege, now gave way to a new idea. Israel was the chosen instrument of Yahweh, but not to achieve a place of dominance among the nations of the world. She was to be a servant, a suffering servant, through which the transforming revelation of God would flow out to regenerate the world.

(3) *A new concept of religion.* Jeremiah laid the foundation for this new concept of personal religion. He had written to the exiles and implied that the Exile was a blessing in making them understand that they could worship God without the institution of the Temple. The Exile popularized this emphasis given by Jeremiah. Let us now look at the basic teachings in the message of Ezekiel.

(1) *The Holiness of God.* Basic in all of the teachings of Ezekiel is the idea that Yahweh is a holy God. Isaiah before him had made this attribute prominent in his message. The passion of Ezekiel is to defend the righteousness and holiness of God rather than to unfold its meaning and thereby make the holy God a lovable God. The nations are to recognize this awful holiness of Yahweh as he displays his almighty power among the nations. "They shall know that I am Yahweh when I send forth my judgments." In Ezekiel, then, God's holiness is closely identified with his physical majesty. The awe-inspiring visions of Ezekiel all underscore this aspect of God's holiness. The nations are destroyed "for his name's sake," that is, for the holiness of God, which is God's honor and majesty, for that holiness must not be profaned in any way.

(2) *Yahweh as Lord of History.* The same idea that Amos and Isaiah set forth, that world history was under the control of Yahweh, is predominant in the message of Ezekiel. In fact, the holiness of Yahweh and the lordship of Yahweh are closely joined in Ezekiel's teaching, for the holiness of God is manifested in

his sovereign rule over Israel and Israel's history. Again and again Ezekiel uses the expression, "In order that you may know that I am Yahweh," which reveals his belief in the transcendent lordship of Yahweh, his sovereignty over all that is human.

(3) *The Problem of Sin, Righteousness, and Retribution.* The fall of Jerusalem and the captivity of the Hebrews brought them face to face with the question of why they were suffering. The people felt that God had not dealt fairly with them, and that they were suffering for sins that were not their own. The complaint against God was expressed in a proverb current in that day: "The fathers have eaten sour grapes, and the children's teeth are set on edge" (Ezek. 18:2). According to this proverb, it seemed as if the innocent suffered, the children for the guilt of their fathers. The nation had been repeatedly guilty of sin and apostasy, and now the generation of Ezekiel's day was bearing the suffering.

Ezekiel had something to say to his countrymen who were troubled by the fact that God had punished guilty and innocent alike for the sins of the nation as a whole. It is not true, he declared, that God treats everybody alike, and punishes good men along with the bad. He deals with individuals. "The soul that sinneth, it shall die."

Ezekiel does not give a full answer, of course, for he does not consider the fact that man cannot be isolated from the group, that no man lives to himself. The fact that innocent people suffer cannot be denied, but what Ezekiel is emphasizing is the responsibility of the individual. He is saying that the people deserved what had befallen them. Every man is rewarded or punished for his own sins. Even though Ezekiel discusses only one aspect of the problem, his emphasis on individual responsibility had a tremendous influence on the development of religion in the later history of the Jewish people. Individual life and conduct came to have a deeper meaning. Emphasis was laid upon individual repentance and the salvation of the soul of man. Men came to understand that God was interested in the welfare of the individual.

(4) *Prophecies Related to Israel's Restoration.* Ezekiel became the pastor of the exiles, going from family to family, giving advice and encouragement. One of the most interesting of his parables of hope is his vision of the valley of dry bones. "Son of man," said God's voice in his heart, "can these bones live?" And I answered, "O Yahweh, thou knowest." And in the vision Ezekiel saw the miracle happen, the dry bones came to life (chap. 37).

Under the symbol of the good shepherd, Israel is again given hope. God will seek out his sheep and restore them to their land. We have here also the promise of the Messianic kingdom, when the Good Shepherd would appear (chap. 34).

The method by which God will redeem his people is pointed out in 36:25-27. When this passage is broken down we find three steps or aspects of the redemptive process: (1) *Forgiveness.* "I will sprinkle clean water upon you, and you shall be clean." Here we have the promise of removal of sin and its guilt. (2) *Renewal, regeneration.* "A new heart I will give you." "I will take out of your flesh the heart of stone." (3) *Aid of the Holy Spirit.* "I will put my spirit within you, and cause you to walk in my statutes." While the prophet's immediate interest was the return of Israel to her own land and the change that would take place in the people upon their return, one cannot but think of these promises as prophetic of the process whereby the new Israel, the church, would come into being.

A picture of the redeemed community is given in chapter 46. Ezekiel was not only the prophet of individualism, but also the priest who saw a redeemed community restored. He recognized that responsible individuals must be related to God's community. In Ezekiel's vision the restored nation, Israel, has now become a church. The details of the vision need not concern us here. The point is that a community of redeemed people, a holy people, a church, now takes the place of the old idea of a holy nation. Here again is a preview of that holy community of the New Testament, the church.

OUTLINE OF THE BOOK OF EZEKIEL

SECTION 3. ISAIAH, PART II (CHAPTERS 40-66)

The greatest of all the voices of hope and courage that spoke to the Hebrew exiles was the author of the second part of Isaiah. He is often spoken of as "The Unnamed Prophet," or "The Prophet of the New Age." We know nothing of his personal history, but his words will live forever. He opened up for the people of Israel new horizons and a world of nations beyond Israel who were to find redemption through Israel, for Israel was to be the servant of Yahweh in this work. Among his most characteristic messages was that of the power and greatness of Israel's God. A hopeless people needed the gospel of a God who was able to save. With biting irony he contrasted the God of Israel with the idols of the heathen; with overwhelming eloquence he sang of the incomparable majesty of Israel's God, and summoned his people to a renewal of their faith.

1. *The Historical Situation.* The prophet's message is addressed to the exiles in Babylon. Israel's captivity is about to end, and the prophet is jubilant over the prospects of an early return to Judah. A summary of the historical developments to this point will aid in understanding the background out of which this prophet spoke.

The name of Cyrus is frequently mentioned in these chapters. While events were fast leading to the downfall of Babylon and the Chaldean empire, Cyrus appeared on the international horizon. His story is one of a swift rise to power and fame. In 550 he became king of Media, and a year later saw him seated upon the throne of Persia. By 546 B.C. he was in control of all of Asia Minor, and in 539 B.C. Babylon fell to him. Thus it was that the Hebrews found themselves captives no longer of Babylon, but of the Persian empire. The exiles must have watched with eager interest the rapid rise to power of this man Cyrus, and often wondered what would be their fate should Babylon fall under his rule.

Deep within the hearts of a minority of the exiles was the hope and expectation that the Day of Yahweh would come, liberate them from captivity, and restore them to their own land. Israel's sense of mission had not been lost to them. When this prophet spoke and interpreted those events of history in the light of God's purpose for Israel and for the entire world, hearts were ready to listen and to take their place in the ongoing purpose of God.

2. *The Prophet and His Ministry.* Although we have no knowledge of the personal history of this prophet, from his writings we may gather a number of things concerning his background and character. His knowledge of events as they were happening would seem to

suggest that he was living in Babylon. He knows well Babylonian life and religion, and speaks as if he were sharing the trials and afflictions of his people.

Paterson speaks of him as "a prophet of profoundest insight. To speak of him as a religious genius does less than justice to his greatness. . . . Perhaps he mingles the character of religious philosopher with that of prophet, but nowhere in the Old Testament do we meet with nobler vindication of the character of God or a more incisive interpretation of the real meaning of redemption. The prophetic inspiration here reaches its apex, and the thoughts here expressed, whatever may have been their original reference, have found their completest and most obvious fulfillment in the words and works of our Lord."[1]

3. *The Date of the Book.* The contents of these chapters indicate that Babylon had not yet fallen. Cyrus had begun his victorious march to power, and the course of events had evidently pointed to the downfall of the Chaldean kingdom. The prophecy, then, can be dated between 549 B.C. when Cyrus became ruler of the Medo-Persian kingdom, and 539 B.C., the date of the fall of Babylon. Students suggest that chapters 40—48 may have been written early in the period of the advance of Cyrus, while chapters 49—55 were doubtless written on the very eve of the fall of Babylon.

4. *The Message of the Book.* The supreme contribution of this prophet to the religion of his people and of the world was his answer to the two most baffling questions which troubled the Jewish exiles—namely, Does God still have a purpose for Israel? and Why does God punish the innocent with the guilty?

(1) *The Servant of God.* Isaiah answers these questions by painting a word-picture, the portrait of the Servant of God. For that Servant of God has a purpose

---

[1]Paterson, *op. cit.*, pp. 192-193.

—a purpose which includes all mankind. Not Israel only, but all men are to be won to a knowledge of the one true God. It is the Servant who will achieve this purpose. Read in Isaiah 49:6 what God says:

> It is too light a thing that you should be my servant
>   to raise up the tribes of Jacob,
>   and to restore the preserved of Israel;
> I will also give you as a light to the nations,
>   that my salvation may reach to the end of the earth.

The mission, however, will not be fulfilled save as the Servant pays a terrible price. He must be a "suffering Servant." These sufferings will not be sent upon him as a punishment; he does not deserve punishment. But only through vicarious suffering can evil men be won to goodness, and atonement be made for sin. Notice Isaiah 53:4-5:

> Surely he has borne our griefs
>   and carried our sorrows; . . .
> But he was wounded for our transgressions
>   he was bruised for our iniquities;
> upon him was the chastisement that made us whole,
>   and with his stripes we are healed.

Who was this Servant? Christians of all ages have interpreted this as a prediction of the sufferings of Christ. It was so interpreted by Philip in his conversation with the Ethiopian eunuch (see Acts 8:34-35).

There are four poems known as the Servant Poems or Servant Songs. (See 42:1-4; 49:1-6; 50:4-9; 52:13—53:12.) In all of these poems the servant is used here to refer to the chosen instrument of God through which his will and purpose are revealed. In these poems, in addition to referring to the individual as explained above, Israel as a nation is looked upon as the servant. Her sufferings were to benefit the world. Also, the faithful remnant of Israel is thought of as a servant. This faithful remnant constituted the servant through which true religion would be kept alive and disseminated throughout the world. But Israel as the servant, and the faithful remnant as the servant, are steps leading to the climax of introducing the suffering Servant of Yahweh as an individual. The Servant is first the nation, then the true Israel or faithful remnant, and finally the One who suffers for the world's sin and misery.

(2) *God as Creator.* In chapters 40—48 we find one of the most magnificent confessions of faith in One God, who is eternal, righteous, and sovereign in his power. But he is also the Creator of heaven and earth.

> Who hath measured the waters in the hollow of his hand
> and marked off the heavens with a span,
> enclosed the dust of the earth in a measure
> and weighed the mountains in scales
> and the hills in a balance (40:12)?

(3) *The God of History.* The prophet characterizes Yahweh as omnipotent and omniscient, with wisdom and power that are unlimited. There was but one sovereign over all; he was the source of all things. (Read 40:25; 41:2-4; 23-24; 46:1-2, 9-11.) It is Yahweh's will that controls the events of history so that his ultimate purpose is fulfilled. This prophet interprets the events of history in such a way to show that Yahweh is the God of history. (See 41:21; 44:28; 45:1; 48:14 which shows Cyrus to be the instrument of God.) To the surrounding nations Cyrus was another military genius bent on conquest, but to the prophet he was the agent of Yahweh, who moved in history, and turned events for his purpose.

(4) *The New Jerusalem.* In chapters 60, 61, 66 we have pictures of Jerusalem as a glorious new city. The city is described in most glowing terms. The beauty and power of this New Jerusalem shall be of a spiritual kind. Salvation was to come out of Zion, for there the Son of God appeared and revealed God's will; outside the city walls he was crucified for the world's sin; in

that city the Holy Spirit was poured out upon the waiting souls; and out of Jerusalem the early apostles and disciples went forth to proclaim the good news into all the world. Jerusalem had indeed become a city glorious.

But in a fuller sense the church, the spiritual Jerusalem, fulfills these glorious prophecies of a new and glorious Zion. The church is now the people of God, the New Jerusalem.

OUTLINE OF ISAIAH (PART II)

SUGGESTIONS FOR FURTHER STUDY

Background Studies
   Snaith, Norman, *The Jews from Cyrus to Herod* (Religious Education Press, 1948).

The Book of Ezekiel
   Robinson, H. Wheeler, *Two Hebrew Prophets* (Lutterworth, 1948). Deals with Hosea and Ezekiel.

See also references under Chapters V and VI.

The Book of Isaiah, Part II

Muilenberg, James, "Isaiah 40—66" in *The Interpreter's Bible*, Vol. V.

North, C. R., *The Suffering Servant in Deutero-Isaiah* (Oxford University Press, 1956).

Rowley, H. H., *The Servant of God and Other Essays* (London, 1952).

See also references under Chapters V and VI.

CHAPTER IX

THE RETURN FROM CAPTIVITY

Ezra-Nehemiah; Chronicles; Haggai; Zechariah;
Obadiah; Malachi; Joel

SECTION 1. GENERAL BACKGROUND

The theme of Ezra-Nehemiah is the history of the return of the Hebrews from their exile in Babylon and the political and religious reorganization of the nation following their return. To understand this period it is necessary to keep in mind three things: the benevolent policy of the Persian rulers toward captive peoples, the depressed economic condition of Palestine, and the continuous hostility of the Samaritans. As you read the biblical books listed at the heading of this chapter, these three things will stand out.

1. *The Decree of Cyrus.* The historical accounts of the conquest of Babylon by Cyrus, inscribed on the Cryus Cylinder, reveal something of the benevolent policy of this ruler in making it possible for captives which the Babylonians had carried to Babylon to be returned to their own land. It speaks of returning to the captive peoples the sacred images which had been taken from their sanctuaries, and then gathering the inhabitants and returning them to their own lands.

The benevolence of the Persian rulers is seen in the decree of Cyrus. This opened the way for the return of the Jews in 538 B.C., sanctioning the rebuilding of the Temple by a later ruler in 520-516 B.C., for another promoting the return of Ezra in 458 B.C. (or perhaps 428 B.C.), and for the return of Nehemiah in 445 and 433.

Ezra tells of the royal decree issued by Cyrus in Ezra

1:1-4 and 6:3-5. The first passage is the decree written in Hebrew and the second in Aramaic, both confirming permission for the Jews to return. Perhaps a better sequence of events will be obtained if the following portions of Ezra and Nehemiah are read in the order listed: Ezra 1—6; Nehemiah 1—7; 11—13; Ezra 7—10; Nehemiah 8—11.

2. *The Return Under Joshua and Zerubbabel.* Ezra 2 speaks of 50,000 returning to the homeland in response to the decree of Cyrus. It may be that at first the number was much smaller and that the 50,000 represents the number that had gone back over a period of several generations. Josephus reports that many of the Jews were hesitant to leave their possessions and return to Judah.

Shortly after the return of the Hebrews they built an altar on the old temple site. They also resumed the offering up of sacrifices which had been discontinued while in Babylon. The Levites were also installed to perform the functions of worship. The second year after their return they laid the foundations of a new temple (Ezra 3). Trouble developed between the Jews and the Samaritans which delayed the work of rebuilding, and for a period of about eighteen years the work was suspended.

The Hebrews experienced a great deal of disillusionment when the promises made in the second part of Isaiah were not fulfilled immediately upon their return. It was difficult for them to understand that the fulfillment was yet future. In the plan of God the time was not yet ripe for the realization of the Messianic hope. The coming of the promised King and his universal kingdom were to find fulfillment in the coming of Jesus Christ.

3. *The Work and Message of Haggai and Zechariah.* In 520 B.C., in the second year of the reign of Darius I (522-486 B.C.), under the leadership of Zerubbabel, a descendent of David, and through the help of the high

priest, Joshua, the work of rebuilding the Temple was started again. It was at this time that two prophets appeared in Judah, who inspired the Jews to go ahead with their task (see Ezra 5). We shall note the messages of these prophets a little later.

4. *The Completion of the Second Temple.* Four years after the foundations of the Temple had been laid, the work was completed and dedicated with impressive ceremonies (Ezra 6:14-22). That was in 515 B.C. The second Temple was a very modest building and could not compare with the splendor of the one built by Solomon. The old men, who had been in Jerusalem and had seen the glory of Solomon's Temple, wept when they saw the foundations of this second Temple laid. Yet, modest as it was, it served as the center of preservation for the faith of Israel. Until Herod the Great designed a new temple on a magnificent scale (20 B.C.), this second Temple was to be the center of the worship of Yahweh for almost five hundred years.

5. *The Hymnbook of the Second Temple.* In the next study we shall make a survey of the Book of Psalms, which has often been called the Hymnbook of the second Temple. Within this Book of Psalms we have the history of Israel's faith from before the time of David down to the very late period in Israel's history. The new restored Hebrew community, with this second Temple as the center, was a worshiping community. It was also a singing community, supported by instrumental and choral music. Who can estimate the value of these psalms in deepening the life and devotion of the Hebrews to Yahweh, and in keeping alive the faith of Israel?

6. *The Work of Nehemiah.* If the coming of Nehemiah to Jerusalem is dated 445 B.C., then we have a period of seventy years from the completion of the Temple to the beginning of his work of reconstruction. There is a great deal of debate with regard to the date

of the activity of Ezra and Nehemiah, and also the sequence in which their books were written. Some are of the opinion that Ezra comes first, about 458 B.C., while others think that Ezra follows Nehemiah and in that case Ezra would be dated 428 B.C. Some would date Ezra even later than 428 B.C. For our purpose we shall think of Nehemiah as coming first, about 445 B.C. and Ezra following him about 428 B.C.

Within these seventy years between the completion of the Temple and the coming of Nehemiah, we have the messages of three prophets. They are: Obadiah, dated about 460 B.C.; Malachi, about the same time (470-460 B.C.); and Joel, sometime between 445-360 B.C. A summary of the messages of these prophets will be given later, but they should be read in connection with this period.

Nehemiah introduced two important reforms which were designed to preserve the identity of the community of Israel and at the same time safeguard the faith of Israel. The first reform was to insist that membership in the Jewish community be based on one's ancestry being traced to Jewish parentage. He was alarmed over the mixed marriages, and especially because the children of such marriages could not speak Hebrew.

Some students of the Old Testament are of the opinion that the *Book of Ruth,* although based on conditions as they existed in the time of the Judges, was written at this time to offset the extreme attitude taken by Nehemiah. The Book of Ruth points out that Ruth, a Moabitess, was the ancestress of David. The Book of Ruth should be read at this point.

The second reform of Nehemiah required that one's standing as a Jew was dependent upon his loyalty to the Torah or Law and his support of the Temple with his tithes. Special emphasis was laid upon the observance of the Sabbath. The real purpose of these regulations was to preserve Israel as a community with a deep conviction of the rich faith she had inherited from the past. Israel always faced the threat of other religions and cultures. Later on, when the Greeks entered Palestine, she had to face this threat again. Writers often criticize this narrow view of Nehemiah, but we must remember that it was within this community, around which these walls of restriction had been erected, that the essential faith of Israel was preserved.

7. *The Work of Ezra.* According to Nehemiah, Ezra brought with him to Jerusalem a copy of "the book of the law of Moses" (Neh. 8:1). He also states that when the people were gathered together on one occasion the book was read to them from early morning until noon. There were later periods of the reading of the Law, followed by a ceremony in which the people renewed their covenant with Yahweh.

Although we cannot be certain of the contents of the book which Ezra brought with him, opinion leans toward the belief that it was the Pentateuch. If so, Ezra was responsible for establishing the Pentateuch as the authoritative standard for the faith and conduct of the Jewish community.

With this review of the developments from the time of the return from Babylon to the end of Nehemiah's second term as governor (about 400 B.C.), let us turn to a brief analysis of the books that come within this period.

SECTION 2. CHRONICLES; EZRA-NEHEMIAH

Ezra and Nehemiah were undoubtedly one book at one time; later it was divided into two books when the Latin translation was made by Jerome about A.D. 400. Actually, however, the scroll containing Ezra-Nehemiah was part of a larger historical work, which included First and Second Chronicles. This is usually referred to as "The Chronicler's History." By noting the beginning of First Chronicles and the ending of Second Chronicles, you will see that the history takes you from

Adam at the beginning down to the decree of Cyrus to permit the return of the Jews to Judah. Ezra-Nehemiah carries the account beyond that point to Nehemiah's second visit to Jerusalem about 400 B.C.

The Books of Chronicles. The books from Genesis to Second Kings gave the history of Israel from the earliest beginnings down to the destruction of the Northern Kingdom in 722 B.C., and of the Southern Kingdom in 587 B.C.

After reading in the Book of Kings about the destruction of Jerusalem in 587 B.C. and of the deportation of the Jews to Babylon, it would seem that the thoroughness of the Babylonian victory should have blasted beyond repair the hopes of Israel for any glorious future. Yet Israel does not lose hope. The prophets had kindled a flame of undying hope. They believed that the Messiah would come; therefore, in the midst of their desolation they found hope.

It is in the books that take form after the Exile (587-539 B.C.), that we find the reasons behind Israel's hope. In the Chronicler's history, written some years after 400 B.C., years after the reign of the last independent king of Judah, we find that the Jews still looked to the Davidic dynasty as the source of Israel's hope for a glorious future. That hope was to be fulfilled in the coming of the Messiah. In the sermons of the prophets of Judah, preached between 740 and 587 B.C., and later collected into books which form part of our Old Testament, the reasons for Israel's hope are to be found.

The Chronicler's history emphasizes the two sources of Israel's undying hope: (1) the Temple in her midst as the guarantee of God's presence with her; (2) the Messiah who is to come and bring to fulfillment the promises made to patriarch and prophet of old.

Who the author of this history was is not known. He is spoken of as the Chronicler. Some have suggested that the author of Chronicles and Ezra-Nehemiah was

Ezra himself. Others have suggested one of the Levites who served in the Temple.

SECTION 3. THE BOOK OF HAGGAI

1. *The Man Haggai*. He was evidently a man of some education. He knew something of what was happening in world affairs, for he showed great interest in political developments. In 2:3 there is the suggestion that he had seen the Temple of Solomon, in which case he would be not less than eighty years old when he wrote this prophecy. Some think he was born in Babylon and educated there.

2. *The Message of Haggai*. His message consists of four brief prophecies. The four messages were written within a period of four months in 520 B.C. Haggai was possessed of a single purpose; he wanted to see the Temple restored and the worship of Yahweh resumed. His messages are designed to inspire the people to set to work at once.

OUTLINE OF THE BOOK OF HAGGAI

I. REBUILDING OF THE TEMPLE STARTED   1: 1-15

II. THE BUILDERS ARE ENCOURAGED   2: 1- 9

III. A PROMISE OF BETTER THINGS   2:10-19

IV. A MESSAGE OF HOPE FOR ZERUBBABEL   2:20-23

SECTION 4. THE BOOK OF ZECHARIAH (PART I)

The Book of Zechariah is often divided into two parts, chapters 1—8 having the same background as the Book of Haggai, and chapters 9—14 belonging to a later period.

Opinion on this twofold division is by no means unanimous. One of the main reasons for dividing the book into two parts is the reference to the sons of

Greece in 9:11. This would be some time after the conquests of Alexander, perhaps during the Seleucid period which began about 312 B.C. If this is the background of chapters 9—14, then they would come later than Zechariah the prophet, whose activity is dated about 520 B.C. There is a great deal to be said for the single authorship of Zechariah. Both Young[1] and Unger[2] write in support of that position.

In this study we are reserving consideration of chapters 9 to 14 of Zechariah for our last chapter.

1. *The Man Zechariah.* Two months after Zechariah delivered his first appeal not to delay the work of the Temple, Zechariah appears to lend aid and support to Haggai. He was a younger contemporary of Haggai, delivering his message in 520 B.C. also.

He was of a priestly family, perhaps one who came up from Babylon with the returning exiles. His name appears in the lists of priests in Nehemiah 12:1, 16. Perhaps he was just a lad when he came out of Babylon.

No priest makes use of the Scriptures as much as Zechariah does. This indicates that the Law and the writings of the Prophets were being recognized as authoritative by the Jews.

2. *The Message of Zechariah.* His message is embodied in eight visions, with chapter 8 giving a summary of his teachings during the period in which the Temple was being reconstructed. Some of the significant passages are as follows:

1:8-17. *The four horsemen.* A symbol of God's control over the affairs of the earth. "The earth resting peacefully" most likely means that Jerusalem has nothing to fear as a result of the conflict of the nations, for those wars have ceased.

1:18-21. *The four horns and the four blacksmiths.*

Horns are used to symbolize power. The number four signifies universality. The powers to be destroyed by the blacksmiths were the nations that had destroyed Judah.

4:1-14. *The lampstand.* This represents the restored Jewish community. The two olive trees are Zerrubabel and Joshua, standing for the spiritual and temporal power in the new community.

5:1-4. *The flying scroll.* This symbolizes the uprooting of the wicked from among the people of God. Emphasis is placed upon holiness as a mark of God's people.

5:5-11. *The woman in the basket.* The wickedness of the Jews uprooted by the flying scroll is to be removed from the community. This removal is symbolized by a woman, who is covered over and carried to Babylon, the symbol of those forces that oppose God.

8:18-23. *The ingathering of the nations.* Here the coming of the nations to God's kingdom is proclaimed by Zechariah.

OUTLINE OF THE BOOK OF ZECHARIAH
(Chapters 1—8)

SECTION 5. THE BOOK OF OBADIAH

This is the shortest book as well as the shortest book of prophecy in the Old Testament. It is made up of twenty-one verses.

The *theme* of the book is the utter destruction of Edom for her treachery, her hate, and her arrogance. Edom was related to Israel, since the Edomites were considered descendants of Esau, as Israel had descended from Jacob. When Jerusalem was being plundered by her enemies, the Edomites helped to capture fleeing Israelites, treated them cruelly, sold them as slaves, and shared in the loot obtained after the city had fallen. Such treachery is the background of the intense wrath and indignation displayed by Obadiah.

The *date* of the book cannot be fixed with any degree of certainty. Harrell points out that it has been dated as early as 889 B.C. and as late as 312 B.C. Then he adds: "On so disputed a point one should not be dogmatic. The author follows those who place the book in the period of the exile."[3]

Recent studies place Obadiah sometime before the destruction of Edom, which took place in the course of the fifth and fourth centuries B.C.[4] Cartledge suggests the best view is to consider the book to have been written about the time of Malachi.[5] This would date it about 460 B.C.

The *message of the book*. The book itself expresses the feelings of the Hebrew people as they come to understand what shall be the judgment and end of their enemy, Edom. The book also denounces all foreign nations and contains a promise of victory for Israel.

Writers often criticize Obadiah as they do Nahum for the intense expression of wrath and judgment against these people. As Nahum announced the fall of

---

[3]Harrell, *op. cit.*, p. 164.
[4]Anderson, *op. cit.*, p. 447.
[5]Cartledge, *op. cit.*, p. 168.

Nineveh, so Obadiah announces the fall of Edom, the bitter enemy of Judah. There is no expression of mercy nor any appeal to repentance. It is all judgment and indignation. For this reason some students feel it does not contain any spiritual message. On the other hand, others have pointed out, and rightly so, that within these cries against Edom's deeds of injustice and seeming joy over her judgment, one can see a force for righteousness at work in the world. "Justice, mercy, and truth; the education of humanity in the law of God; the establishment of his will on earth—these things can be seen behind Obadiah's indignation."[6]

Raymond Calkins sees in this book the antagonism between the religion of the Hebrews and the paganism of Edom and the other nations. Between the two there could be no compromise, but only warfare to the end. Says Dr. Calkins: "It is so that we must interpret the seemingly savage and bitter words of this prophet in order to comprehend their eternal moral meaning. . . . Here we see the never-ending conflict between truth and falsehood, right and wrong, God and Satan. Thus interpreted the book of Obadiah has lasting inspiration for tired and often defeated souls of men in face of inveterate foes that war against their peace and purity."[7]

OUTLINE OF THE BOOK OF OBADIAH

The twenty-one verses, which constitute a single vision, may be divided as follows:

1. The destruction of Edom foretold	vss. 1- 9
2. Why Edom was to be destroyed	vss. 10-14
3. A promise of restoration for Israel	vss. 15-21

[6]G. A. Smith, *The Book of the Twelve Prophets* (Harper, 1928), II, p. 183.

[7]Raymond Calkins, *The Major Message of the Minor Prophets* (Harper, 1947), p. 148.

SECTION 6. THE BOOK OF MALACHI

1. *The General Background.* The period is that between the completion of the second Temple in 515
B.C. and the coming of Nehemiah to Jerusalem in 445
B.C. The days of zeal and fervor that rebuilt the Temple are long past and dead. A spirit of routine and
weariness has set in. The decreasing fervor of the repa-
triates had led to disgraceful negligence on the part of
the priests and to increasing pessimism on the part of
the people. The Book of Malachi, then, most likely
comes out of that period immediately preceding the reforms of Nehemiah and Ezra, probably about 460 B.C.
The evils attacked by Malachi become the object of the
reforms introduced by Nehemiah and Ezra.

According to the book itself, work on the Temple
had been finished (1:7-10), but for some reason the
worship of the Jewish community was lacking in enthusiasm. The Jews had developed a listless and cynical
attitude, and for them religion had lost its glow. It is
suggested that the reason for this attitude may be found
in the developments within Persia. Between 490 and
457 B.C. Persia, who ruled Judah by an appointed
governor, was suffering defeats at the hands of the
Greeks. They were too much occupied with war to pay
much attention to the Jews, who sank back into a state
of careless and wicked manner of living as described in
Malachi.

2. *The Man Malachi.* The name Malachi comes
from the Hebrew word *mal'aki,* which means messenger. A literal translation of the first verse would be:
"The oracle of the word of Yahweh to Israel through
my messenger" (mal'aki). What we know about the
author comes from the contents of the book itself. His
character, his zeal for God and his cause, may be seen
in the message he delivered to the Jewish community at
this time.

3. *The Message of Malachi.* The Book of Malachi

should be read before Ezra, chapters 7 to 10, and Nehemiah, chapters 1—13. The message begins with a declaration of God's love for his people. When the Jewish community is unable to see how God had loved them, the prophet proceeds to give them proof of God's love for them (1:2-5). The prophet then lists the many things of which they had been guilty.

(1) They had neglected the Temple, had placed upon the altar foods that had been polluted, and had offered as sacrifices animals that were blemished. They were offering to God blind, lame, and sickly animals, such as they would not dare to offer to their Persian rulers. Yet they dared to offer them to Yahweh.

(2) Their ritual and worship was only a form and had become a wearisome thing to them. The prophet suggests it would be better to close the doors of the Temple than to carry on such worship which dishonored God. As a result God rejects them and promises a new universal sacrifice, a clean oblation to be offered everywhere among the nations (1:6-14).

(3) He protests against intermarriage with pagans and against divorce (2:10-16).

(4) He charges them with complaining that it is vain to serve Yahweh, for evildoers seem to prosper and come out with the most benefits. In other words, they felt that there should be more tangible evidence of God's love for them in the material benefits which they should but did not have.

Malachi then pleads with them to return to Yahweh, stating that one sign of repentance would be their resuming the obligation to pay tithes to the Lord, a practice they had discontinued. If they did that, God would bless them and they would become great among the nations (3:6-12).

One significant passage is his message in 3:1-5, where the promise is made that Yahweh would send his messenger before he himself would appear in the Temple. In 4:5 it is stated that the messenger will be Elias the prophet (Elijah). Note that although Elias is mentioned by name, Jesus expressly states that John the Baptist, coming in the "spirit of Elias" fulfills the prophecy. (See Matthew 11:14; 17:9-13; Luke 1:17, 76; 7:27.)

OUTLINE OF THE BOOK OF MALACHI

I. THE SINS OF THE PEOPLE AND THE PRIESTS	1: 1— 2:16	
1. The title of the book	1: 1	
2. God's love for his people declared	1: 2- 5	
3. The priests are charged with neglect of the Temple	1: 6— 2: 4	
4. The priests have failed to instruct in the Law	2: 5- 9	
5. The people have been guilty of divorce	2:10-16	
II. GOD WILL COME TO JUDGE AND REWARD	2:17— 4: 6	
1. The day of judgment will come	2:17— 3: 5	
2. A plea for repentance	3: 6-12	
3. The promise of ultimate triumph	3:13-18	
4. The righteous spared in the coming judgment	4: 1- 3	
5. A plea to remember the Law of Moses	4: 4- 6	

SECTION 7. THE BOOK OF JOEL

1. *General Background*. The author does not date his book by any reference to the reigning king or to any definite historical event known to us. Because the data is so limited it is difficult to form any definite conclusions regarding the period which forms the background.

Some students favor a period before the Exile, suggesting that Joel was contemporaneous with Amos or a little earlier. The Hebrews placed Joel between Hosea and Amos in listing the minor prophets, perhaps indicating their belief that the Book of Joel was written early.

There are evidences, however, in favor of a post-exile date. In 3:2 reference is made to the Jews having been scattered among the nations, and in 3:6 they are reported to have been sold to the Greeks as slaves.

This fits in better with the period following the Exile. In addition, the position of the priests and elders as heads of the Jewish community, along with the emphasis upon the ritualistic aspect of religion, all suggest a late date. In that case the book would belong to the same period as does Obadiah and Malachi.

The occasion for this message was a great catastrophe, the visitation of a plague of locusts, accompanied by a severe drought and followed by a famine.

2. *The Man Joel.* Little can be said of Joel, other than what appears in his book. He is aware of his calling as a prophet and as a spokesman for Yahweh. He is aware of God's special and intimate relationship with his people, and sees in the plague of locusts a sign of the day of Yahweh, a day when God would visit his people. In Acts 2:17-21, the Apostle Peter uses the words of Joel to explain the great outpouring of the Holy Spirit on the Day of Pentecost.

3. *The Message of Joel.* The book is divided into two parts. The first part, chapters 1 and 2, consists of two sermons. Joel calls upon the elders, the people, and the priests to pray and to repent in order to avert the coming judgment—the locust plague. The second part, chapter 3, is entirely apocalyptic. It describes the great day of the Lord (3:1-5), God's judgment upon the enemies of Israel (3:6-16), and the coming reign of God (3:17-21).

Attention should be called to the way Joel makes the transition from a *particular day of the Lord* (the locust plague in his own time (chaps. 1—2) to the future Messianic Day of the Lord (chap. 3) in the distant future. The message in the first part was motivated by a definite and calamitous plague, looked upon as a visitation of the Lord, or the Day of the Lord. The message in the second part, pointing to the future when the Messiah would come, was inspired by the continual distress which the Jewish community suffered following the Exile. The prophet's purpose was to encourage the people in a time of discouragement and pessimism with the hope which the future held in the coming of the Messiah.

Evidently the people responded to the message of Joel and returned to Yahweh, for the prophet breaks forth in wonderful words of promise:

(1) "The years which the swarming locust has eaten" would be restored (2:25). The fields would yield their increase and the barns would be filled with plenty.

(2) Yahweh would pour out his Spirit upon all flesh, old and young alike (2:28-32). This is the prophecy which reached its great fulfillment at Pentecost (Acts 2).

OUTLINE OF THE BOOK OF JOEL

I. THE LOCUST PLAGUE, THE DROUGHT, AND THE FAMINE	1: 1-20
II. THE DAY OF THE LORD	2: 1-32
1. The disaster as a sign of the Day of the Lord	2: 1-11
2. Material blessings to follow repentance	2:12-27
3. The promise of his Spirit	2:28-32
III. THE PROMISE OF THE FUTURE	3: 1-21
1. Yahweh's judgment upon the nations	3: 1- 8
2. The judgment of the heathen	3: 9-13
3. The Messianic Age	3:14-21

SUGGESTIONS FOR FURTHER STUDY

Background Studies

Snaith, Norman, *The Jews from Cyrus to Herod* (Religious Education Press, 1949).

Whitley, C. F., *The Exilic Age* (Longmans, 1957).

Ezra-Nehemiah and Chronicles

Anderson, Hugh, *Historians of Israel* (Abingdon, 1962). Presents a survey of the work of the Chronicler.

Anderson, Berhnhard, *Understanding the Old Testament* (Prentice-Hall, 1957). Chapter 14 deals with the work of the Chronicler, including Ezra-Nehemiah.

PART IV: THE WRITINGS

CHAPTER X

THE BOOK OF PSALMS

"Poetry and religion go together," says Julius Bewer. "In moments of religious experience when the soul is one with the eternal harmony of God its utterances often become rhythmic and burst into song; common prose is not adequate to express its joy or its longings; in rhythmic rise and cadence flow forth praise and prayer revealing the deepest feelings and desires."[1]

A large portion of the Old Testament is in poetic form. When the *English Revised Version of the Bible* appeared in 1881, the poetic portions were printed as poetry for the first time. Now all the modern versions of the Scriptures show this poetry wherever it appears in any book of the Old Testament.

The Old Testament books usually classified as poetry are Job, Psalms, Proverbs, Ecclesiastes, Song of Solomon, and Lamentations. A large section of Ecclesiastes, however, is in prose form, while much of Isaiah, Jeremiah, and Ezekiel is in poetical form. Nearly all of the minor prophets are for the most part in poetic form, while poetic sections are to be found in Genesis, Exodus, Judges, Second Samuel, and other books.

SECTION 1. HEBREW POETRY

1. *Rhythm Makes Hebrew Poetry*. Old Testament poetry is characterized by certain rhythmical patterns.

---

[1]Bewer, *op cit.,* p. 340.

As you read the following verse taken from a modern translation of the Old Testament, you will notice something different from the poetry of English writers.

> Ye mountains of Gilboa,
>   let there be no dew or rain upon you,
>   nor upsurging of the deep!
> For there the shield of the mighty was defiled
>   the shield of Saul, not anointed with oil.
>   —2 Samuel 1:21

The one element that makes it poetry and not prose, apart from the feeling with which it is charged, is the rhythm. This is what makes Hebrew poetry.

It was some time before students recognized Hebrew poetry because of this difference. English poetry calls for a certain number of syllables in each line; Hebrew poetry calls for a certain number of accents. The unaccented syllables may be few or many. For instance, read these lines:

> The Lord is my light and my salvation;
>   whom shall I fear?
> The Lord is the stronghold of my life;
>   of whom shall I be afraid?—Psalm 27:1

As you read these lines you naturally give three accents to the first and third lines and two accents to the second and fourth lines. Perhaps the best illustration of this rhythm is to be found in Psalm 29:1, where we have the most common Hebrew line of poetry, having two parts and each part having three beats. Each beat falls on a stressed syllable in the most important word. The stressed syllables are in italics:

> *Give* unto *the Lord*, O ye *mighty*,
>   *give* unto *the Lord* glory and *strength*.

2. *Parallelism.* The most distinguishing feature of Hebrew poetry is its parallelism. A common practice is to have two lines in which the second parallels, sup-

ports, or completes the thought expressed in the first. This greatly enhances the rhythm with a sense of symmetrical balance. The following examples will illustrate some of the types of parallelism.

(1) *Synonymous Parallel.* In this type the idea or thought expressed in the first line of a couplet is repeated in different words in the second line, as illustrated below:

> The heavens are telling the glory of God;
>   and the firmament proclaims his handiwork.
>   —Psalm 19:1

(2) *Antithetic or Contrasted Parallel.* Here the first line is followed by one that has the opposite meaning or stands in contrast with what is stated in the first line, as seen in the following:

> For the Lord knows the way of the righteous,
>   but the way of the wicked will perish.
>   —Psalm 1:6

(3) *Emblematic Parallel.* In this form what is stated in the one line is compared with the other line, thus:

> As a father pities his children,
>   so the Lord pities those who fear him.
>   —Psalm 103:13

(4) *Synthetic or Constructive Parallel.* In this type the second line supplements the thought of the first, or serves to qualify what is said in the first line.

> I cry aloud to the Lord,
>   and he answers me from his holy hill.
>   —Psalm 3:4

3. *Other Characteristics.* A study of Hebrew poetry reveals a number of other peculiarities, of which mention only can be made here. Alliteration, assonance, acrostics, and other artificial forms are to be found.

These features are not brought out in our English translations, in fact, they are difficult to produce in translation. In Psalm 119 we have an example of this elaborate and artificial construction, where there are twenty-two stanzas, each having eight lines. Each of the twenty-two stanzas begins with a letter of the Hebrew alphabet which contains twenty-two letters. In addition, each of the eight lines in each stanza begins with the letter with which the stanza begins.

SECTION 2. THE BOOK OF PSALMS

The Book of Psalms is often referred to as the "Hymnbook of the Second Temple," since it was the Israelite community, following the return from exile, that collected and arranged the Psalter. The second Temple, sometimes called Zerubbabel's Temple, was dedicated about 515 B.C. The leaders of the restored Hebrew community gave special attention to the restoration of worship, and the Psalms became their hymnbook. It is sometimes called "The Praises of Israel," since the Hebrew title, "Tehillim," means praises.

Before the Book of Psalms grew to be the book as we have it today, music and hymns were part of the worship of the Hebrews as far back as David's time. But following the Exile, the religious devotion of the Hebrew people found expression in hymns and praise with both instrumental and choral music. The headings of many of the Psalms point to the existence of musical guilds whose leaders are named in those headings.

This hymnbook played an important part in the preservation of Israel's faith, for in the Psalms we have a summary of Israel's history and her faith from early times. After the return from exile, Israel's faith was nourished through the temple worship, in which the Book of Psalms held such an important place.

1. *Origin of the Book of Psalms.* The Psalms are the product of the distinctive character of Hebrew worship.

"It grew from the aspirations, vicissitudes, humiliations, and hopes of a people who adored God with music and song even in time of distress. It is therefore a poetic expression of that people's religious history during a period of seven or eight hundred years."[2]

Terrien suggests that these Psalms grow out of five distinct characteristics of Hebrew worship, which may be listed as those related to: (1) deliverance in time of warfare; (2) the awareness of the presence of God in their midst; (3) thanksgiving for abundant harvest; (4) the unique or holy history of the Hebrews; and (5) personal communion with God.

Within such experiences, in which God acted to save and bless his people, or in which he manifested himself in a special manner—revelation, understanding, insight into God's character—his will and his purpose for his people were stamped upon the hearts and minds of the participants. Thus the Psalms become not only an expression of the religious experience and worship of the Hebrew people, but records of God's revelation to his people as well.

2. *A Collection of Collections.* The Book of Psalms as a whole is a collection of several collections of psalms. As we now have them, these one hundred and fifty psalms are divided into five books, which may be listed as follows:

Book 1 Psalms 1—41
Book 2 Psalms 42—72
Book 3 Psalms 73—89
Book 4 Psalms 90—106
Book 5 Psalms 107—150

It will be noted that each of the first four books ends with a special doxology. See 41:13; 72:19-10; 89:52; 106:48. The first of these doxologies, Psalm 41:13,

[2]Samuel Terrien, *The Psalms and Their Meaning for Today,* Bobbs-Merrill Co., p. 19.

reads, "Blessed be the Lord, the God of Israel, from everlasting to everlasting! Amen and Amen." It would seem that this verse does not really belong to Psalm 41, but was intended as a conclusion to the collection of psalms in Book 1. In the same way the closing verse of Books 2, 3, and 4 constitute a doxology concluding the book rather than the particular psalm. Psalm 150, the last one in Book 5 is not only a closing doxology for Book 5, but at the same time constitutes a doxology to the entire Book of Psalms. A reading of that last psalm suggests that the compiler of the book is summoning everything that hath breath to praise the Lord.

Before these five books or collections were brought together as we now have them, several collections or "little psalters" were doubtless in separate circulation and use.

3. *Date and Authorship*. The questions of when and by whom the Psalms were written are difficult to answer. Paterson states that "the book as we now have it is the outgrowth of the piety and devotion of countless generations."[3] This means that the writing of the individual psalms covers a period of seven or eight hundred years. G. Ernest Wright would date them from shortly before the tenth century to the fifth century B.C., and suggests that it is not likely that any that are included in our present book were written after the fifth century B.C.[4] Albright "would date the contents of the Psalter in its present form between the eleventh and fourth centuries B.C." Between 1050 B.C. and 400 B.C. would be an approximate date for the writing of these psalms.

As already indicated, these psalms circulated in smaller collections or Psalters before being brought together in their present form. It is also likely that some of the psalms written in an early period, such as those which may have been written by David, underwent

[3]Paterson, John, *The Praises of Israel* (Scribners, 1950), chapter 2.
[4]Wright, *op. cit.*, p. 172.

modification and change through the years before the present collection was complete.

About one hundred of the psalms are ascribed to various persons. Three-fourths of that one hundred, or seventy-five psalms are attributed to David. This means that about half of the collection are linked to his name. The name of Moses appears at the heading of Psalm 90, and that of Solomon for Psalm 72. Psalm 88 is ascribed to Heman and Ezrahite, while Psalm 89 is ascribed to Ethan the Ezrahite. Then there are those which have these headings: "A Psalm to Aspah," and "A Psalm to the Sons of Korah." Several psalms are without names, and these were called "orphan" psalms by the rabbis. Psalm 102 has a very interesting note: "A prayer of one afflicted, when he is faint and pours out his complaint before the Lord."

But it is the name of David that stands out in connection with the psalms, since one half of them are in some way connected with his name. As Moses is the great name in the Law, so David is the great name in the psalms. David was a poet and singer. He planned for the Temple and is credited with the beginnings of the temple choirs, and the musical guilds led by such men as Heman, Aspah, and Ethan. The heading of the Davidic psalms, "To David," does not necessarily indicate authorship. It could mean honorific dedication, or that a particular psalm belongs to a certain collection. The designation of psalms to Aspah and to the Sons of Korah also likely means that they belong to particular collections.

This is not to say that none of the work is that of David. Terrien states that "modern scholarship, after several decades of intensive study, tends to admit that the core of several pieces comes from David himself (1002-962 B.C.) . . ."[5] Paterson also affirms that the Psalter does contain songs of David. It seemed most

[5]Terrien, *op. cit.*, p. 32.

natural, therefore, that the name of David should stand out in connection with this collection of psalms to be used in the worship of the second Temple in Jerusalem.

4. *Classification of the Psalms.* Those who have given careful study to the Book of Psalms have suggested various classifications. All of us are aware as we read the psalms that some express individual thanksgiving, while others express to God the thanksgiving of the entire Hebrew community. We find also that there are psalms of lamentation, both on the part of the individual and the community.

One of the most interesting classifications of the Book of Psalms which has been given wide acceptance is that by Herman Gunkel. He classifies them according to type and theme. While his classification appears to be rather rigid and includes overlapping, a reading of the psalms following this classification will be very helpful. The main types or classes are as follows:

(1) *Hymns, or Songs of Praise.* These would be the hymns for normal worship, and would include such sub-divisions as "Songs of Zion" and "Enthronement Psalms." Psalms included in this group are: 8, 19, 29, 33, 47, 65, 68, 93, 96—100, 103—105, 111, 113— 115, 117—118, 135—136, 145—150.

(2) *Laments of the Community.* These were used in times of misfortune and calamity and include Psalms 44, 58, 74, 79, 80, 83, 106, 125.

(3) *Royal Psalms.* These are psalms which concern the king, including thanksgiving for victory, public intercessions, marriage, and other national occasions. Psalms 2, 18, 20—21, 45, 72, 101, 110, 132.

(4) *Laments of the Individual.* These psalms all reveal the deep emotion of the individual worshiper. Psalms 3, 5—7, 13, 17, 22, 25—28, 31, 35, 38—39, 42—43, 51, 54—57, 59, 61, 63—64, 69—71, 86, 88, 102, 109, 120, 130, 140—143.

(5) *Thanksgiving of the Individual.* Psalms 18, 30, 32, 34, 41, 46, 92, 116, 118, 138.

Gunkel suggests that most of the psalms can be classified under the above five main groups, but states that there are a number of smaller groups or classes of psalms, sometimes only including one or two psalms, which may be listed as follows:

(6) *Blessings and Curses.*
(7) *Pilgrim Psalms.*
(8) *Thanksgiving of the Community.*
(9) *Legends.*
(10) *Psalms dealing with the Law.*
(11) *Prophetic Psalms.*
(12) *Wisdom Psalms.*

Terrien has developed a classification, based on the studies of Gunkel, which is much more appealing for devotional study. It is as follows:

I. HYMNS OF PRAISE
  1. Worship of the Lord of nature
  2. Worship of the Lord of history
  3. Worship of the Lord of Zion

II. PRAYERS IN TIME OF CRISIS
  1. National laments
  2. Personal supplications
  3. Penitential prayers

III. SONGS OF FAITH
  1. Psalms of thanksgiving
  2. Psalms of trust
  3. Psalms of "wisdom" and communion

The following list of readings in the Psalms, arranged according to the nine-group classification of Terrien, will be helpful in understanding the contents of the Book of Psalms.

1. *Nature Psalms.* In these God is worshiped as the Lord of nature. Psalms 8, 19, 29, 104.

2. *The Lord of History.* Here the Hebrew recognizes that God acts in history, and that the ultimate outcome of history is with God. Psalms 46—47, 110, 114.

3. *Songs of Zion.* These are the psalms for the wor-

ship of God as the Lord of Zion. Since the collections were prepared for use in connection with the worship in the second Temple, these psalms reveal the love the Israelite had for the Temple. In Zion was the presence of God, and it was to Zion that the pilgrims returned again and again to worship. Psalms 120 to 134 are Pilgrim Psalms. Psalm 122 is considered the best example of these Pilgrim Psalms. Other Psalms of Zion are 15, 24, 84.

4. *National Laments.* Here the psalms reflect the suffering of the Hebrews as a nation, their penitence in times of crisis, and their hope and faith that God will bring deliverance. As you read these psalms you can imagine the community in penitent humility before God. Psalms 80, 90, 137.

5. *Personal Supplications.* Psalms 22, 42—43.

6. *Penitential Prayers.* Psalms 51, 130.

7. *Psalms of Thanksgiving.* Psalms 65, 103, 107, 124.

8. *Psalms of Trust.* Psalms 23, 27, 121.

9. *Psalms of "Wisdom" and Communion.* The Wisdom Psalms have sometimes been called the Didactic Psalms, because they were composed for purposes of instruction. Sometimes they were arranged as an acrostic, such as in Psalm 119, to help the pupils in memorizing the psalm. Psalms 1, 14, 34, 94, 111—112, 119, 127—128, and 144 are all or in part classified as Didactic Psalms. Psalms 73 and 139 are suggested for reading in this connection.

SECTION 3. RELIGIOUS TEACHINGS OF THE PSALMS

Since the psalms were the outgrowth of the worship experiences of individuals and the worshiping Hebrew community, experiences in which there was a divine-human encounter, it is natural to expect to see emerge in these psalms definite concepts and convictions with regard to God and his being, the nature of man, the problem of sin and suffering, and some hope and expectation with regard to the future life. Here it is possible to give only in bare outline some of the main religious teachings of the psalms.

1. *Concerning God.*

(1) *His Existence.* The psalmist does not try to prove the existence of God; everywhere he assumes that God is. The being of God is so very fundamental to all that the Hebrews believed concerning the world and human existence, that it is everywhere taken for granted. Everything begins with God, as so beautifully expressed in the opening words of the Book of Genesis. Everything begins with God; he is the ground of all being.

(2) *The Nature and Character of God.* The name or names of God used in the Psalms as well as in other books of the Old Testament reveal something of the concept of the nature and character of God as understood by the Hebrews. El and Elohim, along with other forms of the word, are used to refer to God. Without going into the origin of the term, it is generally understood to express "the sublime elevation of God." When used in connection with *Shaddai,* a word whose basic meaning was mountain, we have *God,* the *Almighty.* Thus God is both the "mighty and massive one," as signified by the use of the word derived from mountain, but he is also the one who towers above the world of humanity.

But the term most often used to designate God is *Yahweh.* It is found not less than 6,700 times in the Old Testament, and is translated as Lord, although in the Revised Version it appeared as Jehovah. Although the origin and meaning of the word is obscure, the general view is that it speaks of the One who causes to be what is or what happens. For the Hebrews Yahweh was the One who had stepped into their history and through various acts had brought about their redemption, and who would continue to act on behalf of his people to redeem and save them.

God is eternal, says the psalmist (Psalm 90), declaring that "from everlasting to everlasting thou art God." In Psalm 139 both the omniscience and the omnipresence of God are spoken of, and in many psalms the omnipotence of God is portrayed.

But beyond these attributes, which we speak of as his metaphysical qualities, the psalmist clearly reveals those outstanding moral attributes of God. We have space only to name them, but you will find great satisfaction in hurriedly reading through the psalms and noting where reference is made to such divine qualities as the goodness of God, his righteousness, his justice, his faithfulness, his mercy, and his truth.

(3) *His Self-Revelation.* This God, of whom the Hebrew was so certain of his existence that he never argued the case, had revealed himself to his people in many ways. This self-revelation of God is seen in *nature,* as pointed out in the nature psalms; it also is seen in *history,* as shown in those psalms which recall Israel's history and God's mighty acts of deliverance.

2. *Concerning Man's Relationship to God.* Many psalms picture for us a most intimate relationship existing between man and God. The first psalm portrays the righteous man as delighting in the law of God, and in that law meditating day and night. The same idea is expressed in Psalm 119:97.

But the psalms also reveal *the fact of sin* and the separation that takes place between man and God as a result of that sin. See Psalms 51:3-5; 90:8. A man is made to tremble when he remembers that the hidden sins of his life are known to God.

These same psalms reveal a forgiving God. Penitence and confession on the part of the sinner meets with the response of forgiveness from God. It should be pointed out here what is quite prominent in the psalms, that forgiveness, religion, spiritual life, are things that are *given* by God, not something man earns or wins. In Psalm 40:1-3 this fact is clearly underscored. After all, true religion is not something we achieve ourselves, but something that begins with that which is given us by God in the act of forgiveness and in his receiving us into favor with himself.

3. *Concerning the Future.* There are certain psalms which are known as *Immortality Psalms.* Space does not permit a survey of Hebrew belief regarding death and the future, but Psalms 16, 17, 49, and 73 indicate a breakthrough on the part of Hebrew insight and understanding to an assurance of eternal union with God. As one reads the psalms and traces the development of their thought, he finds the writer or writers emerging with a triumphant faith with respect to the future life. Consider the following verses: "Thou shalt guide me with thy counsel, and afterwards receive me to glory." "As for me, in righteousness will I behold thy face; I shall be satisfied when I awake with thy appearance." "For thou wilt not abandon me to Sheol, nor permit thy loved one to see the pit. Thou wilt show me the path of life: fullness of joy is in thy presence, and pleasures in thy right hand for evermore." These are words which express the faith of the Hebrew psalmists as they look beyond this life and the grave. It is true that we do not have revealed here the New Testament faith in the Resurrection and immortality, but there is expressed the fundamental conviction that he who is joined to God by a living faith is aware that no power, even death, can cut him off from God.

SECTION 4. A UNIVERSAL BOOK

The mission of the psalm writers did not end when the Hebrew nation was crushed beneath the mighty power of a conquering army, nor was the value of their psalms any less when Judaism was overshadowed by an aggressive Christianity that spread throughout the

Roman Empire. These psalms entered into the very life of the early church. In fact, the Book of Psalms was actually the hymnbook of the church of that early period. The hymn which Jesus and his disciples sang on the last night was the Hallel, taken from Psalms 113 to 118. Paul and Silas in prison sang from this book. The first Christian hymns, such as the Gloria in Excelsis, the Magnificat, and the Benedictus in those early chapters of Luke's Gospel, are all fashioned after the psalms.

Such was the quality of the faith and religion of the Hebrews as expressed in the psalms that Christianity has been able to use most of the psalms for these twenty centuries. Today these psalms are sung everywhere around the world.

The psalms are used in the church's worship regularly. Invocations, calls to worship, responsive readings, responses, and doxologies are taken from the Book of Psalms. The psalm became a pattern for the Christian hymn of which there are so many today. What writing is better known than the Twenty-Third Psalm?

The Book of Psalms constitutes the greatest devotional book in our world. The deep insight into the human heart, the understanding of man's struggle with sin and his longing for deliverance, and the spiritual yearnings which find expression in this literature make the Book of Psalms a book for all time. Here in the Book of Psalms, says Martin Luther, we "can look into the hearts of all saints."

SUGGESTIONS FOR FURTHER STUDY

Leslie, E. A., *The Psalms* (Abingdon, 1949).
Oesterly, W. O. E., *The Psalms* (S.P.C.K., 1953). This is a full study of the Psalms.
Paterson, John, *The Praises of Israel* (Scribners, 1950).
Terrien, Samuel, *The Psalms and Their Meaning for Today* (Bobbs-Merrill, 1952).

CHAPTER XI

THE WISDOM LITERATURE

Proverbs; Job; Ecclesiastes

Three important classes of religious leaders in the nation of Israel are referred to in the Book of Jeremiah in these words: "the law shall not perish from the priest, nor counsel from the wise, nor the word from the prophet (18:18). Priest, prophet, and wise man all spoke with the authority of God, and each had his particular spiritual gift. The priest gave the law to the people, which was in the nature of instruction based on the Mosaic faith. The prophet was the spokesman for God and communicated the will of God to the nation as the situation might require. The wise man studied life in an effort to understand its meaning, and from his years of experience and his knowledge of the accumulated wisdom of the past, he gave his counsel. This wisdom or counsel the wise men put into written form, which we know today as the Wisdom Literature. Thus it was preserved through the centuries for teaching and instruction of the people of God.

Section 1. The Meaning of Wisdom

In the Book of Proverbs we are told that "the fear of the Lord is the beginning of wisdom" (9:10). Here the word "fear" does not imply that one is frightened by God; rather, it means awe, reverence, humility, and the proper attitude which the creature should hold toward the Creator.

Our word "philosophy" comes from the Greek and means "the love of wisdom." The Greeks were earnest seekers after wisdom, and their literature, as well as the literature of other peoples, reveals the deep longing they had for wisdom. Their search for wisdom was, in fact, a search for the meaning of life. It is in this sense that the writers of the Old Testament Wisdom Literature use the word. In the light of this explanation we could very well read Proverbs 9:10 as follows: "The fear of the Lord is the beginning of understanding the meaning of human existence."

The writers of the books of the Wisdom Literature have as their basic conviction that life comes to have meaning and significance only as it is filled with faith in God and as it follows the purpose he has for human life. These men wrote with the authority of God, even as the prophet spoke with the authority of God. (See Jeremiah 18:18.) As the prophet's special *charisma* or gift enabled him to interpret the meaning of God's action and to communicate the divine will to the people, so the special *charisma* enabled the wise men to interpret for the people the meaning of life and human existence in the light of what the Law and the Prophets had taught. A study of the books of the Wisdom Literature will reveal that to those who wrote those books wisdom was "not mere human insight, but is the divine purpose by which the universe is directed, and in obedience to which man should order his life."

SECTION 2. THE WISDOM LITERATURE OF THE OLD TESTAMENT

The Old Testament books of Wisdom Literature which form part of the canon are Proverbs, Job, and Ecclesiastes. There are also wisdom sections to be found in the Psalms and in the writings of the prophets. Outside of the Old Testament canon there are books, written during the second century B.C., known as "The Wisdom of Ben Sira" (Ecclesiasticus), and "The Wisdom of Solomon."

Sometimes the Wisdom Literature is divided into

two classes, one of which gives practical instructions on how to live a good and successful life, as well as to find happiness. The Book of Proverbs is a sample of this type of literature. The second class seeks to discover the meaning of life. Man is encompassed with suffering and tragedy and he asks the reason why. Ecclesiastes and Job are books of this second type. Perhaps we should look at the literature as a whole and see in it attempts to interpret the meaning of life in different situations in the light of the basic teachings and convictions found in the Law and the Prophets.

SECTION 3. THE BOOK OF PROVERBS

1. *Authorship and Date.* The Hebrew Massoretic manuscripts give the name of this book as the "Proverbs of Solomon." Students today cannot be sure of what portions of the material in Proverbs comes from Solomon. Some are of the opinion that those found in the oldest section of the book come from Solomon.

There are six sections of the book where authorship is mentioned. In addition to the name of Solomon, we find Agur, Lemuel and the "wise men." (See 10:1, 22:17, 24:23, 25:1, 30:1, 31:1.) After a study of the titles to the six sections of the book, Young expresses his viewpoint as follows:

From a survey of these indications, it will be seen that the book does not claim in its entirety to be the work of Solomon. On the other hand, there is no reason for doubting the trustworthiness of these titles and not assuming that the bulk of the book is indeed from Solomon.[1]

Since Solomon was noted for having written many proverbs (1 Kings 4:32), the entire book came to be attributed to him by the Hebrews.

Our Book of Proverbs in its present form is general-

[1]Young, Edward J., *An Introduction to the Old Testament,* p. 301.

ly considered to have been prepared about the time of Ezra, though the collection of such proverbs was in process as far back as the time of Solomon, at least.

2. *The Meaning of "Proverb."* The Hebrew word *mashal* means more than what we usually mean when we speak of a proverb. In English it is used in the sense of a maxim, such as "a word to the wise is sufficient." But the Hebrew meaning goes beyond that and contains also the comparison or symbolic saying, even the form of the parable as we have it in the New Testament. The earliest proverbs we know about are single-line sentences, but the most characteristic form of the literary proverb is the couplet, such as the following:

> A wise son makes a glad father:
>   but a foolish son is a sorrow to his mother. (10:1)

> Like vinegar to the teeth, and smoke to the eyes,
>   so is the sluggard to those who send him. (10:26)

3. *Divisions or Collections.* An analysis of the book reveals seven divisions or collections. Some suggest there are eight collections, making two collections out of number three, listed on page 190.

(1) Chaps. 1—9. "The proverbs of Solomon." These are a series of loosely connected discourses.

(2) Chaps. 10:1—22:16. "The proverbs of Solomon." A collection of individual proverbs or wise maxims in couplet form.

(3) Chaps. 22:17—24:34. "Words of the wise." Practical advice and warning, as from father to son. (Chap. 24:23-34 is sometimes listed as a separate collection.)

(4) Chaps. 25—29. "These also are proverbs of Solomon which the men of Hezekiah king of Judah copied."

(5) Chap. 30. "The words of Agur son of Jakeh of Massa."

(6) Chap. 31:1-9. "The words of Lemuel, king of Massa."

(7) Chap. 31:10-31. A poem in praise of a virtuous woman.

4. *Selected Proverbs*. The proverbs are not classified in the book itself, so in order to read them intelligently and with appreciation, one must learn to sort them out and classify them. Here are some of the general headings for classification, with references for typical examples in each.

(1) Business problems. 6:6-11; 18:17; 22:26-27, 29; 24:30—34; 28:19

(2) Problems of parents and children. 10:1; 23:13-24; 30:17

(3) When friends have quarreled. 17:9; 26:20.

(4) Warning against exaltation over riches. 11:28; 13:7

(5) Strong ethical teachings. 22:1

(6) Social relationships. 13:20; 14:29; 17:9-17; 25:21; 27:10

(7) Home life. 18:22; 19:14; 22:6, 15; 23:13; 31:10

(8) Righteous living. 14:34; 25:21-22

(9) Stewardship enjoined. 3:9-10

(10) Concerning the penalty for evil. 23:29-32

(11) In praise of woman. 31:10-21

5. *Basic Teachings of the Book of Proverbs*. Behind the proverbs found in this book there are some basic teachings which may be summarized here.

(1) *Concerning Religion*. Since this book deals so much with practical precepts and moral conduct, some have thought that it does not contain much that is religious. This is to overlook what is the major premise of the book, in fact, what one might call the text of the entire book: "the fear of the Lord is the beginning of wisdom." As has already been pointed out, fear means reverence, awe, humility, and the proper attitude of the creature toward the Creator. True wisdom begins when

one bows before God and acknowledges His sovereignty over one's life. In this book God is regarded as supreme and absolute in power, creator and controller of the whole earth. It would seem, also, that the expression "the knowledge of God" as used by Hosea and Jeremiah, and "the fear of the Lord" refer to the same thing. Man must come into a personal relationship with God in order to understand the true meaning of life.

(2) *The Seriousness of Life.* The writer is not pessimistic, but there is an intense seriousness about his writing (14:13). The wise man is one who has trained himself to discern between good and evil; to seek after an ideal and an objective such as God might set up. As a man must learn to control his appetites, so he must control his time and energies, must arrange his life so that it is in accord with the highest good.

(3) *Concerning Marriage and the Home.* The standard of marriage is that of monogamy. The seventh chapter of Proverbs gives a very graphic warning against sexual vice. The deadliness of sexual sins is pointed out in chapters 5 and 6.

Proverbs also has a great deal to say about the home, children, and discipline. Home is pictured as a kinship group, with father, mother, children, and the aged of a former generation. (See 13:1, 24; 17:6; 19:18; 22:6, 15; 29:15, 17.)

(4) *Concerning Goodness.* Perhaps we can gain some idea of goodness in this book by looking at some of the qualities it exalts.

Humility: 11:2; 15:33; 16:5; 18:12; 22:4
Self-control: 14:17; 16:32; 17:27-28; 18:13
Veracity: 10:10; 12:22; 13:5; 16:6; 19:22
Kindness: 11:17; 12:10; 21:21
Generosity: 11:25; 22:9; 28:25
Justice: 21:15; Fidelity: 25:13

(5) *Why Be Good?* Perhaps the teaching of this book on this point may be summed up as follows:

Wickedness leads to disaster, whereas moral conduct has the favor of God.

(6) *What Is the Meaning of Life?* The meaning and significance of life are always found in God. Life is the reward of those who reverence God (19:23; 22:4).

SECTION 4. THE BOOK OF JOB

The Book of Job is the crowning masterpiece of the Wisdom Literature. All of these writings are in poetical form, but the Book of Job is the greatest of them all. It is considered to be one of the world's greatest poems. Carlyle said of it: "One of the grandest things ever written with pen. . . . A noble book; all men's book. . . . Sublime sorrow, sublime reconciliation; oldest choral melody as of the heart of mankind; soft and great as the summer midnight, as the world with its seas and stars. There is nothing, I think, in the Bible or out of it, of equal literary merit." Tennyson pronounced it "the greatest poem whether of ancient or modern times." Both in thought and style the poetry of the book is wonderful.

1. *Authorship and Date.* A wide difference of opinion exists with regard to the date of this book. A study of the poetic sections of the book has led some students to conclude they were not written before the seventh century B.C. Dr. Pfeiffer would place the poet at the time of Jeremiah (605-580 B.C.); Terrien dates him between 580 and 540 B.C.

Conservative opinion, expressed by Young, would date the book during the reign of Solomon (961-922).[2] Then, after surveying the various viewpoints and pointing out how varied they are he concludes:

If the unity of the book be granted, then it would seem that the Solomonic age was as fitting a time for its composition as any. At the same time it must be admitted that, as we have it, certain

[2]Young, *op. cit.,* p. 309.

portions, *e.g.*, the prologue, may exhibit a more recent linguistic revision. If so, this would account for some of the grammatical constructions of the chapter, which seem to be reflections of a later period. But this is difficult to determine.[3]

Nothing definite can be said with regard to the identity of the author. It is assumed that he was one of the wise men among the Hebrews, though some are of the opinion that he was an Edomite. The central figure is Job, a patriarch who lived in the land of Uz, or Idumea. The name of Job was one that was very common in the patriarchal period (2000—1500 B.C.) and in Ezekiel 14:14-20 reference is made to a Job known for his righteousness.

2. *Purpose and Theme of the Book.* Traditionally it has been held that the theme of the book is the dark and difficult problem of why innocent people suffer. It paints for us the utter loneliness and misery of a man who, because of the teaching that all suffering is a punishment for sin, feels himself cut off from God and men. However, students are coming more and more to feel that the problem of why the innocent suffer provides only the occasion for the consideration of a much deeper question. Anderson suggests that the theme of the book is *the character of man's relationship with God.*[4] Irwin looks upon the book as a description of Job's experience as *a pilgrimage of faith and hope.*[5] Continuing, Irwin says: "From an initial theology not unlike that of his friends, he moves on under the spur of their taunts, first into deep pessimism and rebellion, then gradually to a dawning hope which through notable apprehensions of faith comes to clarity in his great affirmation, 'He knows the way that I take; when he has tried me, I shall come forth as gold' (23:10)."

G. Ernest Wright states that "Job was written to ex-

[3]*Ibid.*, p. 313.

[4]Anderson, *op. cit.*, p. 491.

[5]Irwin, William A., *The Wisdom Literature, The Interpreter's Bible*, I, p. 217.

plode the common notion of the wise men, and for that matter of most pagan peoples of the time, that deity rules the world in a moralistic way, so that one can assess his goodness in the sight of God on the basis of his prosperity."[6] And again, "The formula of the wisdom movement cannot explain all suffering. The reason is that *there is mystery in* God's dealing with men, and in the last analysis no human formula is capable of resolving the mystery completely."[7]

Perhaps all three views expressed above enter into the theme and purpose of the book. It is "a pilgrimage of faith and hope," in which "the character of man's relationship with God" stands out, but the critical problem of suffering in a world controlled by a God of absolute goodness and power provides the question which leads to an understanding of the nature of the pilgrimage and of the relationship to God.

3. *The Book of Job as Drama.* The book is written in semidramatic form. Some writers have suggested that it is modeled after the Greek drama. The dramatic appeal of the book is in the intense thought expressed in the dialogue. The reader of the book sees himself in the experiences of Job, who is a man of like passions with the reader and with all human beings. The fierce conflict in which the poem pictures these passions fill it with dramatic appeal.

4. *The Story the Book Tells.* Perhaps we can best understand the book by looking briefly at the story. The central figure is Job, a patriarch who lived in the land of Uz. He was both pious and prosperous. Into all this prosperity and happiness Satan enters to accuse Job. He declares that Job is serving God for what he can get out of that service. Satan is given permission to disturb Job's prosperity and to afflict him bodily. As a result his prosperity is destroyed, his children die, and

⁶Wright, *op. cit.,* p. 181.
⁷*Ibid.,* p. 188.

he is afflicted with a grievous and loathsome disease. He is in a sad state. The news of his misfortune spreads to other lands and brings from afar three men of note, who come to be his comforters. When these three men see Job's distress and suffering, the fountain of their speech is sealed and they sit in silence for seven days and nights. This is the soliloquy of friendly silence.

After this the dialogue begins, each friend consoling, then trying to explain the reason for Job's distress, and then denouncing Job for his failure to acknowledge that his trouble has come upon him because of sin which he refuses to acknowledge and confess.

None of this is able to bring from Job any acknowledgment of sin or transgression, for he is conscious of his own innocence. As the dialogue proceeds we find Job's friends speaking three times, and three times Job answers them. In the beginning they are sympathetic and weep at the sight of his suffering; yet they can see no solution to his problem unless he confesses his sin. These are their words:

> If iniquity be in thy hand, put it far away,
>   and let not unrighteousness dwell in your tents.
>   —Job 11:14

It is a difficult struggle for Job, and in the end he finds peace. But not before he is faced with severe temptations. He is tempted to denounce God and then resign himself to his misery. He feels that he is innocent but that God destroys the innocent and guilty alike. He is also tempted to doubt the fundamental justice of God's dealings with men, and he desires only the opportunity to present his case in person before God. In chapter 19:25-27 you can see that Job's confidence is returning and that he is sure that divine justice will finally prevail.

The climax of the drama is reached in chapters 38—41, when God answers out of the whirlwind. These verses hold up to scathing derision man's idea that his puny intellect can penetrate the deep mysteries of the universe. God makes clear that a problem like Job's is too difficult for him to solve and he must leave it with God, who will do all things well and for his own purpose. His reply to God is given in 42:2-6. G. Ernest Wright summarizes the climax as follows:

"He was, like so many people, one who had only heard of the Lord by the hearing of the ear, but 'now mine eye sees thee.' One cannot use his individual sufferings to deny the manifold evidence in God's world of his goodness. Without the goodness of God in creating and sustaining the world, man indeed would have no hope. Finally, the very fact that God chose to appear before Job is an act of grace. Job is comforted, not because he has an intellectual understanding of God, but because his own eyes have seen God and he can trust even where he cannot understand."[8]

5. *Summary of the Dialogue.* Since the entire discussion centers around the problem of suffering and why evil is allowed, the five answers given to the question may be summarized as follows:

(1) The first answer is that of Satan. Suffering or evil comes to test a man whose goodness is shallow or superficial. Satan charged that Job was serving God because of the good things that came out of that service.

(2) The second answer is that of the two friends. Suffering and evil come upon a man to punish him for his sin, whether he recognizes that sin or not.

(3) The third answer comes from Job. Yielding to doubt and temptation, he says that suffering and evil come because God is unjust.

(4) The fourth answer comes from Elihu. He declares that evil and suffering come to warn or to educate or to discipline.

(5) The final answer comes from God, who speaks

[8]*Ibid.*, p. 188.

out of the whirlwind. Suffering is mystery. It will always remain a partial mystery, since our knowledge is always partial. But the wisdom of God satisfies Job and he finds peace.

OUTLINE OF THE BOOK OF JOB

SECTION 5. THE BOOK OF ECCLESIASTES

The name Ecclesiastes is Greek for the Hebrew word or title, *Qoheleth* or *Koheleth*. The Hebrew term evidently refers to one who addressed an assembly, from which we get our English translation of "The Preacher." The English translation of "preacher" should not lead us to conclude that the central figure in the book was a preacher in the modern sense. Rather, he was one of the wise men whose lectures and discourses have been brought together in this single volume.

1. *Authorship and Date*. The author was likely the head or leader of a group of sages known as the wise men. He speaks of himself as "king over Israel in Jerusalem," and his message as "the words of the Preacher, the Son of David, king in Jerusalem" (1:1-13). The reference is to Solomon, the wise man *par excellence,*

and the context of the book suggests that he is an old man with the experiences of life behind him.

Admittedly this reference is to Solomon, even though the word "Solomon" is nowhere used in the book. On the basis of the above reference, as well as to other references that could refer to Solomon without mentioning his name, some hold to Solomon as the author. Until the time of the Reformation there was a general tradition that Solomon wrote the book, but Martin Luther felt the evidence was against such a conclusion. Since that time the more general opinion leans toward an authorship other than Solomon.

Young, who speaks for the conservative point of view, states that the book is later than the time of Solomon, perhaps should be dated about the time of Malachi.[9] Others think it may have been written as late as 300 B.C.

2. *Purpose and Theme of the Book.* Earlier in our study of the Wisdom Literature it was pointed out that the wise man sought to understand the meaning of life and existence, and to interpret that meaning for the people. The writer puts himself in the position of one who is finding it difficult to discover any meaning at all in life. He has been labeled among other things: a skeptic, a pessimist, a hedonist, a materialist and, in recent times, the earliest existentialist. He is really not any of these for the simple reason that he is a man of faith. He believes in the reality of divine providence (3:11, 14-15; 8:17; 11:5). He speaks in praise of divine wisdom (7:12, 19; 9:13-18), and points to the coming of divine judgment (3:17; 11:9; 12:13-14). We should keep these convictions in mind if we are to understand Ecclesiastes. He opens the book with words which may be thought of as his thesis:

> Vanity of vanities, says [Koheleth] the preacher,
> vanity of vanities! all is vanity.

[9]Young, *op. cit.*, p. 340.

The word "vanity" is a translation of a Hebrew word meaning "nothing" or "nothingness." One modern writer has rendered the expression "vanity of vanities" as "the absolute absurdity of it all." The ideas of uselessness and transitoriness are also implied by the Hebrew word.

Notice how the author pursues this theme:

1. All man's labors are vain. (1:4-11)

2. Wisdom only leads to more perplexity. (1:12-18)

3. Pleasure brings no enduring satisfaction. (2:1-12)

4. The wise man as well as the fool ends up in the grave. (2:13-17)

5. The pursuit of wealth is like chasing the wind. (2:18-26)

6. Life becomes monotonous as a result of the unchanging order of events, there is nothing new and life becomes weary. (3:1-3)

7. The uncertainty of the future hangs like a cloud over the present. (3:14-22)

Thus he pursues his theme to the end of the book. He examines life and does not find it very satisfactory. To him, the realities of life do not correspond to the yearnings of the heart. His deepest desires are thwarted by the hard facts of human existence. He is aware of his own restlessness, but knows nothing about what Augustine experienced when he said, "Our hearts are restless, O Lord, until they rest in thee." He has yet to experience what every true Christian has experienced in Christ, that the longing after true satisfaction in every man's heart finds fulfillment in our union with God.

3. *The Message of the Book.* In outlining the purpose and theme of the book, something of the message was indicated. The writer is saying that this world, this life, all its pleasures, all its wonders cannot satisfy the

restless heart of man. As Job was concerned with human suffering, so Ecclesiastes is concerned with happiness in life. Actually, he is dealing with the value of life. He looks at life from different angles. Sometimes he sees only the dark side, while at other times he sees the brighter side. He seems to be deeply conscious of the fact that the good in life does not measure up to the yearnings and expectations he has. This man concluded there was little use in trying to penetrate the mysteries of life. His last word, which suggests the leap of faith, is: "Fear God, and keep his commandments; for this is the whole duty of man" (12:13-14).

Perhaps here is where we may summarize a few of the topics with which the writer deals.

(1) *The Meaning of Life and Death.* He is concerned because he has such a short time to live in this world and discover the meaning of human existence. He has no answer to the problem of death, such as the Christian finds in the promise of the Resurrection. The book literally cries out for some revelation on the future-life. The Book of Daniel shed some light for them (Dan. 12:2-3), but it was Jesus Christ who brought immortality to light through the gospel. However, because he was deeply conscious of the shortness of life and had been unable to find a satisfactory answer to the problem of death, he is dead serious about life and how it is to be lived.

(2) *The Author Believes in God.* With all of his pessimism, he reveals a strong belief in the sovereignty of God. It is this God who controls and orders all things, but how he exercises his sovereignty is something one cannot know. To him, therefore, God was transcendent, but not immanent; he was the high and lofty one whom many could not approach. God was beyond human understanding, therefore his purposes and his ways were not open to man's understanding. It was left for Jesus to bring man and God together in a most intimate fellowship.

OUTLINE OF THE BOOK OF ECCLESIASTES

SUGGESTIONS FOR FURTHER STUDY

General Introduction

Robinson, T. H., *The Poetry of the Old Testament* (Duckworth, 1952).

Irwin, William A., "The Wisdom Literature" in *The Interpreter's Bible*, Vol. I, pp. 212-219.

Paterson, John, *The Wisdom of Israel* (Abingdon, 1961). This is an introduction to the Books of Job and Proverbs.

The Books of Job, Proverbs and Ecclesiastes

Fritsch, Charles T., "Proverbs" in *The Interpreter's Bible*, Vol. IV (Abingdon Press, c. 1955).

Hanson, Anthony and Miriam, *The Book of Job* (S.C.M. Press, 1953).

Robinson, T. H., *Job and His Friends* (S.C.M. Press, 1954).

Terrien, Samuel, "Job" in *The Interpreter's Bible*, Vol. III (Abingdon Press, c. 1955).

Toy, C. H., *A Critical and Exegetical Commentary on the Book of Proverbs* (Scribners, 1904).

Ginsberg, H. L., *Studies in Qoheleth* (New York, 1950). A Jewish study of Ecclesiastes.

Gordis, R., *The Wisdom of Ecclesiastes* (New York, 1945).

CHAPTER XII

THE CLOSE OF THE OLD TESTAMENT

Jonah; Esther; Zechariah (Chapters 9—14);
Daniel; Song of Solomon

The ultimate fulfillment of God's purpose for Israel was not realized in the reconstructed community that emerged as a result of the work of Nehemiah and Ezra. The history of the Hebrew people, as far as the Old Testament records are concerned, ends with the work of Nehemiah and Ezra at approximately 400 B.C. The first book of Maccabees, not in the Old Testament canon, gives us information concerning events during the second century B.C. Between Ezra and the historical information given in the first book of Maccabees, little is known of what was happening in the Jewish community. However, the Book of Jonah, Esther, Zechariah (chapters 9—14) and Daniel throw some light on the situation and developments during this period. It is supposed that the Jews were living in peace and security during that time. However, the peace was not to endure for any length of time, for revolution and war were soon to engulf the tiny kingdom. Things were soon to happen in international affairs that were to have a direct bearing on Israel's future and the fulfillment of God's purpose for her as his chosen people. The writings we shall look at in this study bring us to the close of the Old Testament. At the same time they serve as a bridge between the Old Testament and the New Testament.

SECTION 1. GENERAL BACKGROUND

1. *Conflicting Views.* In our study of Ezra-Nehe-

miah it was pointed out that those reforms were designed to build an exclusive Israelite community, whose
basic motive was to insure preservation of the community as the people of God as well as to preserve the essential faith of Israel. That there was some opposition
to the program of Ezra-Nehemiah was evident, and
the story of Ruth was used at the time to modify the
extreme position of Jewish exclusiveness. We come
now to consider two books which present opposing positions; they are the Books of Jonah and Esther.

2. *The Book of Jonah.* Although the background of
this story is that of the days of Jeroboam II (2 Kings
14:23-25) who reigned in the eighth century B.C., during which period Jonah, the son of Amittai lived, the
story itself was doubtless written during the period following the time of Ezra-Nehemiah, sometime after 400
B.C.

Nineveh, as the excavations show, was a very great
city. Jonah was commissioned to preach to Nineveh,
warning them of destruction. Jonah fled from such a
task, for the Assyrians were bitterly hated by the Jews
for their cruel oppressions. In a miraculous way Jonah
was brought back to the city and proclaimed the message of Yahweh. When in mourning, the Assyrians actually did extend the fast and sackcloth even to their
animals as mentioned in Jonah 3:7. Their repentance
resulted in the city being spared.

The purpose of the Book of Jonah is to provide a
mirror in which its readers will see themselves as they
really are—petty, selfish, unreasonable men, unwilling
to admit that God's love extends to all men and not
only to the Hebrew people. Israel had learned that
God's threats against her could be revoked by repentance; the Book of Jonah taught her that God would
act in a similar manner toward the Gentiles. God was
interested in other peoples, even those who had been or
were enemies of the Hebrews and who had opposed
God's purposes. The outstanding message is God's love

and care for all men, Gentiles and Jews. Thus the message of Jonah takes its stand alongside of the teachings of the second part of Isaiah, where the light is to go to the Gentiles in order that the uttermost parts of the world may come to know of Yahweh's purpose and salvation.

3. *The Book of Esther.* The background of this book is laid during the Persian period (486-465 B.C.), but was doubtless written late in the Persian period when the Jews were persecuted because they resisted efforts to be assimilated within the empire. Back of this refusal to be assimilated was the conviction that they were a chosen community with a definite mission. Haman is the leader in a massive program against the Jews of the dispersion, but his plans fail through the loyalty and courage of Mordecai and Queen Esther, who risks her life to save her people. Instead of the Jews suffering, their persecutors were put to death. A festival of rejoicing which followed the deliverance of the Jews is now known as the Feast of Purim, in commemoration of the *pur* or lot that Haman had cast to determine the day of vengeance.

The atmosphere of this book is similar to that which is felt in Ezra-Nehemiah. One senses that an effort is made to preserve the essential distinctiveness of the Jewish community and its faith. In so doing, they seemed to lose sight of the wider view of God's purpose in seeking the salvation of the whole world. The author's purpose is to make clear God's providential care for his people. This is, perhaps, its principal message.

SECTION 2, THE GREEK PERIOD

The rise of Alexander the Great (336-323 B.C.) brought Greece and Greek culture and influence into Palestine. The Persian empire of the time of Nehemiah has gone. It is a new world, for it breathes a new atmosphere, the atmosphere of Athens. Alexander crossed

over into Asia Minor in 334, defeated the Persians in
Syria in 333, and in 331 triumphed over them in Mesopotamia. The way was then open for him through
Persia into Afghanistan and on to the Indus river in
what today we know as West Pakistan. All of this was
accomplished by 327 B.C. Alexander died at Babylon
in 323 B.C.

Alexander was also interested in the spread of Greek
culture, for it was one of the dreams of the Greeks that
their culture should spread to every land. The leaven of
Hellenistic culture continued to work, and in the last
centuries before Christ gradually permeated the major
part of the Mediterranean world including Palestine. In
due time Greek became the second language of the
country. Many cities acquired Greek names. Greek ar-
chitecture was borrowed for public building, Greek
philosophy was taught in the schools, and Greek customs became part and parcel of public and private life.

The term "Hellenism" was applied to the Greek influence and culture as it spread throughout the empire.
Alexandria in Egypt became one of the chief centers of
Greek influence, where a great library was established,
as well as other facilities for the disseminating of Greek
learning. This spread of Greek influence led to the use
of the Greek language as the medium of communication. This was not the classical Greek, but a
vernacular or everyday language known as *koine*
Greek.

After the death of Alexander his empire was gov-
erned by his generals and successors. Palestine came
under the rule of the Seleucids of Syria, while Egypt
came under the Ptolemies. During the centuries that
followed the death of Alexander, Palestine shuttled
back and forth as a subject province under Syria and
Egypt, or under the Seleucids and the Ptolemies.

It was under Ptolemy II (285-246 B.C.) that the
translation of the Hebrew scriptures into Greek was
begun. This translation was known as the Septuagint.

In Egypt the Jews, whose spoken language was Aramaic, soon adopted Greek as their language.

It was not long after the death of Alexander before Palestine came under the rule of the Ptolemies, along with Egypt. Things were pleasant for the Jews, who were given a great deal of liberty. Many of the Jews welcomed the Hellenistic culture.

SECTION 3. PERSECUTION UNDER ANTIOCHUS EPIPHANES

The Seleucid empire was founded by Seleucid I (305—281 B.C.). Periodically Palestine was controlled by the Seleucids. In 223 B.C. Antiochus III, known as the Great, became ruler of Syria. He waged continuous war against Egypt, and in 198 B.C. gained a decisive victory which brought Palestine under the rule of Syria and the Antiochus dynasty.

Antiochus was zealous for the spread of Greek culture. This brought the Jews into conflict with his policies. Even while Palestine was under the rule of Egypt, loyal Jews were opposed to those who submitted to the Hellenistic influences. A Jewish sect known as the Hasidim, who were the forerunners of the Pharisees of a later period, aroused the nationalistic hopes of many for the establishment of a Jewish state. These zealous Jews emphasized the Torah and were violently opposed to those who went along with the Greek ways.

When Antiochus IV (175-163), known as Epiphanes, came to the throne, the Jews found themselves involved in conflict which led to suffering and bloodshed. Based on his claims of divinity, Epiphanes exercised absolute authority and sought in every way possible to integrate Greek culture throughout his domain. Coins were cast with the image of Antiochus and inscribed with the Greek word *theos,* meaning god. Tolerance was granted the various peoples in his kingdom to worship their own gods and to follow their religious customs, provided an act of worship to Zeus was carried out. This would in effect be a symbol of their submission to the absolute authority of Antiochus.

This brought the Jews into immediate conflict. In 169 Antiochus IV pillaged the Temple. A year later, when it became apparent that the religious Jews would not submit voluntarily to Hellenization, he decided upon the use of force. A Syrian army partially destroyed Jerusalem, and a Syrian garrison was installed on the hill west of the Temple. There soon followed a systematic persecution aimed at destroying the Jewish faith. Regular sacrifices at the Temple were suspended and Jews were no longer permitted to observe the Sabbath and their regular feasts. It became a crime to possess copies of the Scriptures or to circumcise Jewish children. Pagan altars were set up throughout the land and Jews who refused to sacrifice swine's flesh upon these altars were liable to death. In December 167 B.C., the cult of Olympian Zeus was instituted in the Temple, an altar was set up to Zeus, and Jews were compelled to take part in the pagan festivities. This was, perhaps, the first systematic religious persecution in history. Judaism was severely tested, but it withstood the test and bequeathed to us the heritage of the Old Testament.

The test, however, was more than the external persecution of Antiochus and the Seleucids. The real test was in the struggle to preserve the true faith of Israel against the attractions of pagan Hellenism. This ideological struggle between Judaism and Hellenism began long before the persecution by Antiochus IV, and lasted long years after it. Hellenism spread rapidly and made itself felt in the Temple, among the priests and even the high priest himself.

In the years that followed many Jews apostatized from the faith of Israel. In contrast, however, the severe persecutions endured by the Jews brought out many who remained faithful unto death. They were the martyrs and saints, the true Israel of God, the spiritual heirs of those seven thousand who did not bow their knee to Baal in the time of Elijah.

SECTION 4. THE MACCABEAN PERIOD

Out of the conflict described in the preceding section came a revolt that led to the independence of the little kingdom of Judah until Jerusalem was taken by the Romans under Pompey in 63 B.C.

The revolution began in 167 B.C., when Mattathias, the priest of a small village near Jerusalem, slew a Jew who was offering a sacrifice to Zeus and the Syrian soldier who had ordered the sacrifice to be offered. With his five sons, Mattathias fled to the hills and challenged all who were faithful to the Law and the Covenant to follow him. Upon his death in 166 B.C., his son Judas, who was given the title of Maccabeus, meaning hammer, was commissioned to continue the campaign of revolt. The army of Judas was successful and a treaty with Antiochus followed. On December 25, 165 B.C., he rebuilt the altar of the Temple, and service in the Temple was resumed. Although war continued under the direction of each of the brothers, the independence achieved lasted for about one hundred years.

SECTION 5. THE BOOK OF ZECHARIAH, PART II (CHAPS: 9—14)

Attention has already been called to the fact that chapters 9—14 of the Book of Zechariah evidently belong to a period later than chapters 1—8. A study of the first eight chapters reveals a writer who uses the first person singular quite freely and carefully dates each prophecy. His references to persons and events show that he lived at the same time as Haggai and wrote those chapters during the period of the restoration and rebuilding of the Temple (520-515 B.C.).

Beginning with the ninth chapter, the center of interest is no longer restricted to the struggling post-exilic community, but embraces the broader scene of Israel and the world and perhaps the end of time.

The author is anonymous and, except in one chapter, the first personal pronoun is not used. No date is indicated, and there is no clear reference to persons or events by which a date may be fixed. The style is more formal than that of the first part, which is simple and direct.

The message is addressed to the Jews during one of their periods of fierce conflict. It was not likely during the Persian period, for they displayed only a mild interest in the Jews. An invasion along the coastal plain is referred to in 9:1-7, which doubtless points to the route taken by Alexander in his conquest of 322 B.C. In the same chapter the Greeks are mentioned as enemies of the kingdom of Judah. This would suggest that these chapters were written after the Greeks had become masters of Palestine, perhaps about 300 B.C. There are some significant passages in these chapters to which attention should be called:

The Messianic King. 9:9-10. (See Matt. 21:5; Mark 11:1; Luke 19:29; John 12:14.)

The Rejection of the Good Shepherd. 11:4-17. The prophet takes God's place as the good shepherd and is rejected by the leaders of the people. He receives for his wages thirty pieces of silver. (See Matt. 26:15; 27:9.) Read 13:7-9 after 11:4-17.

The Piercing of the Servant of Yahweh. 12:10. The one who is to be pierced is not identified, but the author's style suggests the Servant of Yahweh in Isaiah 52:13—53:12. John's Gospel sees the fulfillment of this prophecy in the piercing of Christ's side on the cross (19:37).

The Purifying Fountain. 13:1-7. Matthew 26:31 suggests the fulfillment of this passage in Christ, at least by way of accommodation.

The conflict between the paganism of the Greeks

and the religion of Yahweh, which flared into a period of bloody struggle under Antiochus IV, provides the background for these chapters. This unnamed prophet who wrote these chapters was confident that Yahweh would save Jerusalem by some supernatural means. (Read 9:13-16.) Through this message the prophet points to the coming of the Messianic King, whose dominion shall be from sea to sea, and through whose reign people of all nations shall worship the King, the Lord of Hosts. (See 9:9-10; 14:16.) The Gospel of Matthew identifies Zechariah's Messianic King with Jesus Christ.

SECTION 6. THE BOOK OF DANIEL

The Book of Daniel belongs to a class of literature called "Apocalyptic." The Book of Revelation in the New Testament belongs to this same type of literature. In Ezekiel, Zechariah, Joel, Isaiah, and Amos there are sections which are written in the same style and which also belong to this type of literature we call apocalyptic, a term derived from the Greek word *apokalyptein,* meaning to uncover, disclose, reveal.

In this type of literature, picture language or symbolic language was used to communicate God's message. Both Daniel and Revelation were written to nerve the people of God to remain loyal to him and his truth in periods of mounting persecution. By the use of these symbols and imagery the meaning was veiled from the oppressors, but clear to those of the faithful who were familiar with the symbolic vocabulary. These books unveiled for the people of God an infinite God, mighty to save, who would bring his people ultimate victory and triumph.

1. *Fundamental Ideas in Apocalyptic Literature.* It was the problem of Jewish apocalyptic writers to reconcile the disasters then facing the nation with the power and justice of God. If God, the Creator of the

world, is righteous and if he exercises his sovereignty over all the world, how can the facts of evil in human experience and society be reconciled with the universal reign of this righteous God? The Jewish mind naturally thought of what their ancient leaders and prophets had promised them as a nation. Those promises were not yet fulfilled, for they were under a foreign rule. They had faced disappointment after disappointment and defeat after defeat. This was their problem then: How can this continued persecution and oppression be explained in the light of the fact that the Jewish nation was the chosen of God? God must still love his people. Daniel answers this question by pointing out that the power of God as manifested in the past will be manifested again in a greater and more powerful way to bring victory and triumph for the kingdom of God. The fundamental ideas behind this literature may be summed up as follows:

(1) *The Kingship of God.* He exercised his sovereignty over all the world. His kingship was universal, and was manifested in mighty acts of power. Psalm 145:9-13 gives a very beautiful picture of the universal kingship of God.

(2) *Evil and Good in Constant Conflict.* All the Jewish writers of apocalyptic literature saw and pictured evil and good in constant conflict in the lives of men and nations.

(3) *Judgment.* Because God's kingdom is everlasting, and also righteous, there must in the end come a judgment upon the wicked. The justice of this universal sovereign required that evil be punished. The age-long struggle between good and evil would end finally, and righteousness and goodness and truth would triumph.

(4) *A Philosophy of History.* These fundamental ideas found expression in a very clear philosophy of history. The Jewish writers believed that the events of history, though pictured in dramatic form, were under the control of God. They believed that the order and

sequence of events in human history had meaning. The meaning was that history is marching onward to a clearly defined goal. To them, the ultimate outcome of history was under the control of Yahweh, the sovereign ruler of the universe. They expressed their belief that behind the course of human events is a purpose, and that there is a higher righteous power to which all events of history ultimately must be subservient. The evil forces of the world may be victorious for a time, but finally they must bow to God, the sovereign ruler.

Behind the Book of Daniel one discovers these same four fundamental ideas.

2. *The Date of the Book of Daniel.* Considerable discussion continues to center around the date of the writing of this book. There are two main schools of thought on this point. One point of view insists that it was written during the Exile, with some suggesting a date between 537 and 500 B.C. This is because the first chapters describe incidents and visions experienced by Daniel the sage and prophet during the Exile in Babylon.

The other point of view suggests that the book was written or edited during the period when the Jews were under the rule of the dynasty of Antiochus, especially Antiochus IV (Epiphanes), about 175—165 B.C. The purpose of the book, then, would be to nerve the faithful Hebrews during the period of intense persecution to be loyal and faithful to Israel's faith. The stories which tell of the faithfulness of Daniel and his friends during the period of Babylonian exile would serve to challenge the people during this later persecution under Antiochus to exhibit a similar courage and loyalty. In a similar manner the Book of Revelation in the New Testament was designed to give strength and courage to the people of God during the period when the Roman demand for emperor worship would lead to the death of multitudes of loyal Christian believers.

However, both Daniel and the Book of Revelation

go beyond the immediate period of persecution for which they were written, and point to the future when, at the end of history, ultimate triumph comes to the kingdom of God.

3. *The Message of the Book of Daniel.* In the discussion of the fundamental ideas behind apocalyptic literature, and in the section dealing with the date and purpose of the Book of Daniel, something of the message of the book was stated. Space does not permit a detailed interpretation, but the following résumé of two types of interpretation will guide the reader in further study.

PART 1. CHAPTERS 1—6

These are the chapters which recount the experiences of Daniel and his friends while in exile in Babylon. Whether the book was written early or late, they are designed to arouse courage and loyalty on the part of the persecuted people of God.

Chapter 2 calls for some special consideration, since it is apocalyptic in nature. The four parts of the great image the king saw in his dream, the head of gold, breast and arms of silver, thighs of brass, and legs and feet of iron and clay, were interpreted to mean four successive universal kingdoms that would arise. One type of interpretation applies the four parts of the image to Babylon, Media, Persia, and the Graeco-Syrian kingdoms. Identified with the fourth part is Antiochus IV, the great persecutor of the Jews. Following the fourth kingdom the Messianic kingdom would emerge, symbolized by the "stone was cut from a mountain by no human hand" (2:45). In the last years of the following century (4 B.C. the Messianic king was to be born in Bethlehem. (Antiochus IV is dated from 175-164 B.C.) Another type or method of interpretation makes the head of gold represent Babylon, to be followed by Persia, then by Grecian kingdom and finally by the Roman kingdom. In the days of the fourth or Roman kingdom, Jesus Christ, the Messianic king was born and the kingdom of God emerged on the scene, like a stone hewn from the mountain without hands. The ultimate triumph of the kingdom of God throughout the world is symbolized by the stone becoming a great mountain, filling all the earth. Such a prospect for the kingdom of God would challenge the Hebrews in the midst of their temptations and persecutions to be loyal to Yahweh's Law and to the faith of Israel.

PART 2. CHAPTERS 7—12

The second part is made up of four visions of an apocalyptic nature.

Vision 1. Chapter 7. This parallels that of chapter 2. In this vision four beasts are chosen to represent the same kingdoms as are represented by the four parts of image. In verses 15-17 it is stated that the beasts stand for four successive world powers. When the power of these dominions is broken, there appears one to whom dominion and power is given, whose dominion would be both universal and everlasting. This vision is given an interpretation similar to that of chapter 2. One method of interpretation looks upon the four beasts as representing the Babylonian, the Median, the Persian, and the Grecian kingdoms, with the little horn referring to Antiochus IV (Epiphanes), who so severely opposed the Jews in their worship of Yahweh, as already explained in a previous section. The independence gained by the Jews under the Maccabees, which enabled them to reestablish the worship of God, is interpreted to be the fulfillment of the vision.

The other method of interpretation makes the four beasts represent Babylonia, Medo-Persia, Greece, and the Roman kingdoms, followed by the establishment of the kingdom of God when the "one like unto the son of man" appeared.

Vision 2. Chapter 8. Two beasts appear in this vision, a ram with two horns, interpreted by the angel to be a symbol of the Medo-Persian kingdom, while the he-goat is explained to represent the Grecian kingdom. The notable horn is identified as Alexander the Great, under whose military exploits the expansion of the empire took place. With the death of Alexander, his kingdom was divided into four parts, symbolized by the four horns that arose in place of the one. Out of one of these horns or divisions arose a little horn which became very great. This is usually identified as Antiochus IV (Epiphanes) whose antagonism toward the Jews and their worship of Yahweh is aptly described in the actions attributed to the little horn. See the section of this chapter dealing with the general background of this period.

Vision 3. Chapter 9. This vision is concerned with seventy weeks of years in which the fortunes of the Temple and its worship, the coming of the Anointed One, and the destruction of the city and the sanctuary. One method of interpretation takes the 490 years as an approximate period of time, rather than an exact one. It interprets the period to reach from King Zedekiah to the restoration of worship under Judas Maccabeus (587 to 165 or 164 B.C.). A second method of interpretation would make this period stretch from 457 B.C. to A.D. 33. In this case the return of Ezra, followed by Nehemiah, is dated at 457 B.C. The sixty-nine weeks or 483 years end in A.D. 26, which is the year of the baptism of Jesus, the Anointed One or Christ. In the midst of the last week or the seventieth week, the Anointed One was cut off, or crucified, thereby making an end of sin by his atonement.

Vision 4. Chapters 10—12. These chapters are interpreted to apply to the development of the political power and struggle in Egypt, Syria and Palestine, culminating in the rise of Antiochus IV (Epiphanes), his persecution of the Jews, and of his passing from the scene of action. The vision culminates in the rise of Michael, who may stand as a symbol of Christ, the Messiah, the shepherd of his people. A time of trouble is pictured followed by resurrection. The kingdom of God reaches fulfillment at the end of history.

Whatever method of interpretation may be followed in interpreting the symbols of an apocalyptic book like Daniel, the basic teachings or principles underlying such literature are the most important things to be kept in mind. These have already been given. The several interpretations applied to these visions clearly show that history is under the control of God and that its ultimate outcome is determined by Him. It was this conviction that nerved the Jewish remnant to be faithful and loyal to the faith of Israel, and to preserve for the generations to come the knowledge of the revelation that had come to them through many generations of faithful men and women.

Section 6. The Song of Solomon

The opening verse of the book gives it its title: "The Song of Songs, which is Solomon's." Like "Holy of Holies" and "King of Kings," this is a Hebrew form of the superlative.

Because Solomon's name appears in the book several times, tradition has attached his name to it as the author. Young[1] does not see any sufficient reason for doubting the authorship, while others feel it is not the work of a single author but represents a collection of songs handed down from generation to generation. As we have the book today it is generally thought to be a collection prepared or edited after the Exile, but using

[1]*Op. cit.*, p. 323.

songs that go back as far as the ninth century B.C. or earlier.

The Hebrews regarded the Song of Solomon as something very sacred, as indicated by the statement of Rabbi Aquiba at the Synod of Jamina in A.D. 90: "All the scriptures are sacred, but the Song of Songs is the most sacred of all." Thomas Aquinas, during the last days of his life, worked on a commentary of the Song of Solomon. The general background of the book is to be found in those passages of the Old Testament in which the covenant relations between God and his people are likened to the relations between a husband and wife. (See Hosea 1—3: Jeremiah 3:1-6; Isaiah 58:4-8.)

The Song is made up of a number of dialogues, which for the most part take place between the bride and the bridegroom. There is also some dialogue between the bride and the daughters of Jerusalem.

Very early the Hebrews interpreted the book as an allegory. They saw in it a reflection of the history of the nation from the Exodus to the Messianic restoration. Yahweh's love for Israel was the central thing in this book for the Hebrews.

The Christian church accepted this allegorical interpretation of the songs and saw in them the love of Christ for the Church and the love of the Church for Christ. This has perhaps been the dominant view and is reflected in the chapter headings of the King James Version.

A number of Catholic scholars take a literal interpretation of the songs but in addition give them a typical meaning, pointing out that they reveal the love of Christ for the Church.

Young, a conservative Old Testament student, takes the position that the book is didactic and moral in purpose.[1]

[1]*Ibid.,* p. 327.

The Song does celebrate the dignity and purity of human love. This is a fact which has not always been sufficiently stressed. The Song, therefore, is didactic and moral in purpose. It comes to us in this world of sin, where lust and passion are on every hand, where fierce temptations assail us and try to turn us aside from the God-given standard of marriage. And it reminds us, in particularly beautiful fashion, how pure and noble true love is. . . . the book may be regarded as a tacit parable. The eye of faith—as it beholds this picture of exalted human love—will be reminded of the love that is above all earthly and human affections—even the love of the Son of God for lost humanity.

The following outline will be helpful in reading the book:

I. The Prologue. 1:1-4
This introduces the theme and the main characters.

II. The bride's search and discovery. 1:5—2:7

III. The bridegroom comes, departs, and is found again. 2:8—3:5

IV. The bridegroom extols the beauty of the bride. 3:6—5:1

V. The bride is not ready for the bridegroom when he appears; she later goes in search of him. 5:2—6:3

VI. Final dialogues between the bride and the bridegroom. 6:4—8:7

VII. The bride and her brothers. 8:8-14

SECTION 7. BETWEEN THE TESTAMENTS

The Old Testament ends with the Messianic hope and the glories of the Messianic age yet to be realized. The fulfillment of these prophetic expectations were to be realized in the coming of Jesus Christ, the establishment of his kingdom and his church, and their expansion throughout the world. This is the story that unfolds in the New Testament period. Before that story unfolds, there were religious and political developments which should be summarized here. This will form a bridge between the Old and the New Testaments.

1. *Political Developments.* Although the Maccabean revolution gave independence to Judah, there was continuous struggle with Syria and others. Simon Maccabeus, the son of Mattathias expanded the borders of the small Jewish kingdom. At his death his son, John Hyrcanus assumed the title of king as well as that of high priest. He conquered Idumaea, the ancient Edom, and compelled the people to accept the Jewish faith, thereby becoming members of the Jewish community. In 128 B.C. he conquered Shechem and destroyed the Samaritan temple built on Mount Gerizim about 350 B.C. (See John 4:4-29.)

After the death of John Hyrcanus in 103 B.C., the next forty years were filled with conflict and bloodshed. This led to intervention on the part of Rome in 63 B.C. when Pompey took Jerusalem and Judah came under the rule of Rome. In 37 B.C. Herod the Great, an Idumaean became the political ruler of Judah under the Romans. In the eighteenth year of his reign, about 20—19 B.C., Herod began the construction of a new temple in Jerusalem for Jewish worship. In John 2:13, 23 it states that at that time forty-six years had elapsed since the work had started. Herod the Great died in 4 B.C., and Jesus was born sometime before the death of Herod.

2. *Religious Developments.* Within the Jewish community religious or theological differences arose. These differences resulted from differences in the interpretation of the Law and its application to contemporary life. These differences were reflected in the parties or sects which arose.

(1) *The Pharisees.* The most important of these religious groups was the Pharisees, who continued the tradition of the Hasidim of the Maccabean period. The Hasidim had opposed the inroads of Greek culture when Judah came under the rule of the Greeks. The Pharisees emerged as a distinct party about the middle of the second century B.C. They were very strict in their

practice of those regulations which set the Jews off as a separate and distinct people, such as the observance of dietary rules, circumcision, fasting, prayer. In addition to the Pentateuch, they accepted "the tradition of the elders" known as the oral law. This mass of oral tradition was later codified as the *Mishnah* (second law). The oral tradition of the Mishnah needed explanation and interpretation, and the Mishnah with its explanations was called the *Gemara*. These form the *Talmud*. The Pharisees believed in the resurrection of the body, in angels, and placed a great deal of emphasis on the coming of the apocalyptic kingdom. The Pharisees did not favor revolt against foreign rule, differing therefore from another group or party among the Jews known as the Zealots, who favored the fostering of active revolt against foreign domination.

(2) *The Sadducees.* They were the most conservative party of the Jews, both politically and religiously. They held strictly to the Torah or Law as the only source of divine authority, and refused to accept the oral traditions that had grown up around the interpretation of the Law. They belong to the priestly aristocracy and the secular nobility of Jerusalem. In contrast to the Pharisees, they rejected the belief in the Resurrection, future rewards, angels, and demons, and most of the apocalyptic speculations. They followed a policy of collaboration and compromise with the powers controlling Judah.

(3) *The Essenes.* During the period when Palestine was subjected to continual pressure from outside, one group of Jews, known as the Essenes, withdrew from society in order more fully to fulfill what they believed was Yahweh's purpose for them. They lived ascetic lives in community centers, some in towns and some in the open country. They conceived themselves to be the true Israel, the remnant through whom God was going to fulfill his purposes. They practiced community of

goods, disapproved of marriage, and followed a strict discipline.

(4) *The Qumran Community.* In 1947 there was discovered at Qumran in the wilderness of Judea near the Dead Sea a number of scrolls, now called the Dead Sea Scrolls. The discovery was followed by excavations which disclosed what was the ancient headquarters of a Jewish religious community. At first scholars referred to the sect as "the Covenanters," but now it is generally recognized that the community was the Essene sect, or closely related to it. It was at this center that the members produced the Dead Sea Scrolls.

There are two groups or categories of the Dead Sea Scrolls. One group consists of the books of the Old Testament included in the Old Testament canon. The second group is made up of noncanonical books. Most of those in this second category were written by members of the religious community and give us information concerning their religious ideas. Prior to these discoveries at Qumran, no Old Testament manuscripts written before the beginning of the Christian era were known.

Space allows only limited mention of several significant things which follow from the discovery and study of the biblical manuscripts found among the Dead Sea Scrolls.

(a) *Significance for the Canon.* With the exception of the Book of Esther, at least a fragment of every book in our Old Testament has been discovered in the Qumran caves. Whether the absence of the Book of Esther indicates the Qumran Community did not accept it as canonical or whether copies of it are merely lost, is still a question. The discovery of these scrolls and fragments represents another confirmation of our Old Testament Canon of thirty-nine books.

(b) *Significance for the Text.* The Hebrew text of the Old Testament, which was transmitted by the Jewish scholars known as the Masoretes, in the sixth to tenth centuries A.D., and known as the Masoretic text, was thought to be the closest to the original text. The discoveries at Qumran have led scholars to feel that there was a proto-Masoretic text which was used by the Qumran scribes in preparing the scrolls. W. F. Albright holds the position that the presence of this proto-Masoretic text at Qumran supports the tradition that the older books of the Old Testament were edited during the Babylonian exile and brought back to Palestine during the sixth and fifth centuries B.C. If Albright's position is confirmed, it would mean that we have a link with an older Old Testament text and gets us closer to the original writers of some of the books.

(c) *Significance of the Isaiah Scroll.* This scroll, which contains the entire Book of Isaiah, is known as the St. Mark's scroll. It contains correct ancient spellings of Assyrian names. Albright suggests that this was a copy that had been brought from Babylon, about 150 to 100 B.C. "One wonders" says Millar Burrows, whether it was itself made in Babylon." Here we have an ancient text adding confirmation to the text and contents we have depended upon.

(d) *Significance for Future Translations.* Future translations of the Old Testament are certain to be affected by the Qumran discoveries. The St. Mark's scroll of Isaiah, one of the first biblical scrolls found at Qumran, was discovered in time to influence the Revised Standard Version's translation of Isaiah in a few passages.

With this we come to the close of our Old Testament study. For the Jews their hopes waited for fulfillment in the future. Such was the situation when Jesus came preaching "the kingdom of God is at hand." With that message he initiated the new age in fulfillment of the prophetic utterances of the Old Testament.

SUGGESTIONS FOR FUTURE STUDY

General Background

Oesterly, W. O. E., *The Jews and Judaism in the Greek Period* (S.P.C.K., 1941).
Snaith, Norman, *The Jews from Cyrus to Herod* (Religious Education Press, 1949).

Apocalyptic Literature
Frost, Stanley, *Old Testament Apocalyptic* (Epworth, 1952).
Rowley, H. H., *The Relevance of Apocalyptic* (Lutterworth, 1947.)

The Book of Daniel
Heaton, E. W., *The Book of Daniel* (S.C.M. Press, 1956).
Kempin, Albert, *Daniel for Today* (Warner Press, 1952).
Smith, F. G., *Prophetic Lectures on Daniel and the Revelation* (Gospel Trumpet Co., 1941).